THE
CONQUEST OF BREAD

BY

P. KROPOTKIN

AUTHOR OF " FIELDS, FACTORIES, AND WORKSHOPS"
"THE MEMOIRS OF A REVOLUTIONIST," ETC,

ISBN: 978-93-5128-993-7(HB)

First Published in 1906
Indian Reprint in 2017

Published by

Kalpaz Publications
C-30, Satyawati Nagar,
Delhi – 110052
E-mail: kalpaz@hotmail.com
Website: kalpazpublications.com
Ph.: +91-9212142040

CONTENTS

PREFACE 7

1. OUR RICHES 13
2. WELL-BEING FOR ALL 21
3. ANARCHIST COMMUNISM 29
4. EXPROPRIATION 37
5. FOOD 47
6. DWELLINGS 66
7. CLOTHING 74
8. WAYS AND MEANS 77
9. THE NEED FOR LUXURY 83
10. AGREEABLE WORK 94
11. FREE AGREEMENT 100
12. OBJECTIONS 111
13. THE COLLECTIVIST WAGES SYSTEM 124
14. CONSUMPTION AND PRODUCTION 136
15. THE DIVISION OF LABOUR 141
16. THE DECENTRALIZATION OF INDUSTRY 144
17. AGRICULTURE 152

PREFACE

ONE of the current objections to Communism, and Socialism altogether, is that the idea is so old, and yet it could never be realized. Schemes of ideal States haunted the thinkers of Ancient Greece ; later on, the early Christians joined in communist groups ; centuries later, large communist brotherhoods came into existence during the Reform movement. Then, the same ideals were revived during the great English and French Revolutions ; and finally, quite lately, in 1848, a revolution, inspired to a great extent with Socialist ideals, took place in France. " And yet, you see," we are told, " how far away is still the realization of your schemes. Don't you think that there is some fundamental error in your understanding of human nature and its needs ? "

At first sight this objection seems very serious. However, the moment we consider human history more attentively, it loses its strength. We see, first, that hundreds of millions of men have succeeded in maintaining amongst themselves, in their village communities, for many hundreds of years, one of the main elements of Socialism—the common ownership of the chief instrument of production, the land, and the apportionment of the same according to the labour capacities of the different families ; and we learn that if the communal possession of the land has been destroyed in Western Europe, it was not from within, but from without, by the governments which created a land monopoly in favour of the nobility and the middle classes. We learn, moreover, that the mediaeval cities succeeded in maintaining in their midst for several centuries in succcssion a certain socialized organization of production and trade ; that these centuries were periods of a rapid intellectual, industrial, and artistic progrcss ; and that the decay of these communal institutions came mainly from the incapacity of men of combining the village with the city, the peasant with the citizen, so as jointly to oppose the growth of the military states, which destroyed the free cities.

The history of mankind, thus understood, does not offer, then, an argument against Communism. It appears, on the contrary, as a succession of endeavours to reaUze some sort of communist organization, endeavours which were crowned with a partial success of a certain duration ; and all we are authorized to conclude is, that mankind has not yet found the proper form for combining, on communistic principles, agriculture with a suddenly developed industry and a rapidly growing international trade. The latter appears especially as a disturbing element, since it is no longer individuals only, or cities, that enrich themselves by distant commerce and export ; but whole nations grow rich at the cost of those nations which lag behind in their industrial development.

These conditions, which began to appear by the end of the eighteenth century, took, however, their full swing in the nineteenth century only, after the Napoleonic wars came to an end. And modern Communism had to take them into account.

It is now known that the French Revolution, apart from its political significance, was an attempt made by the French people, in 1793 and 1794, in three different directions more or less akin to Socialism. It was, first, *the equalization of fortunes*, by means of an income tax and succession duties, both heavily progressive, as also by a direct confiscation of the land in order to subdivide it, and by heavy war taxes levied upon the rich only. The second attempt was to introduce a wide *national system of rationally established prices of all commodities,* for which the real cost of production and moderate trade profits had to be taken into account. The Convention worked hard at this scheme, and had nearly completed its work, when reaction took the overhand. And the third was a sort of *Municipal Communism* as regards the consumption of some objects of first necessity, bought by the municipalities, and sold by them at cost price.

It was during this remarkable movement, which has never yet been properly studied, that modern Socialism was born—Fourierism with L'Ange, at Lyons, and authoritarian Communism with Buonarotti, Babeuf, and their comrades. And it was immediately after the Great Revolution that the three great theoretical founders of modern Socialism—Fourier, Saint Simon, and Robert Owen, as well as Godwin (the No-State Socialism)—came forward ; while the secret communist societies, originated from those of Buonarotti and Babeuf, gave their stamp to militant Communism for the next fifty years.

To be correct, then, we must say that modem Socialism is not yet a hundred years old, and that, for the first half of these hundred years, two nations only, which stood at the head of the industrial movement, i.e. Britain and France, took part in its elaboration. Both—bleeding at that time from the terrible wounds inflicted upon them by fifteen years of Napoleonic wars, and both enveloped in the great European reaction that had come from the East.

In fact, it was only after the Revolution of July, 1830, in France, and the Reform movement of 1830-2, in this country, had shaken off that terrible reaction, that the discussion of Sociahsm became possible for the next sixteen to eighteen years. And it was during those years that the aspirations of Fourier, St. Simon, and Robert Owen, worked out by their followers, took a definite shape, and the different schools of Socialism which exist nowadays were defined.

In Britain, Robert Owen and his followers worked out their schemes of communist villages, agricultural and industrial at the same time; immense co-operative associations were started for creating with their dividends more communist colonies ; and the Great Consohdated Trades' Union was founded—the forerunner of the Labour Parties of our days and the International Workingmen's Association.

In France, the Fourierist Considerant issued his remarkable manifesto, which contains, beautifully developed, all the theoretical considerations upon the growth of Capitalism, which are now described as " Scientific Socialism." Proudhon worked out his idea of Anarchism, and Mutualism, without State interference. Louis Blanc published his Organization of Labour, which became later on the programme of Lassalle, in Germany. Vidal in France and Lorenz Stein in Germany further developed, in two remarkable works, pubhshed in 1846 and 1847 respectively, the theoretical conceptions of Considerant ; and finally Vidal, and especially Pecqueur—the latter in a very elaborate work, as also in a series of Reports —developed in detail the system of Collectivism, which he wanted the Assembly of 184S to vote in the shape of laws.

However, there is one feature, common to all Socialist schemes, of the period, which must be noted. The three great founders of Socialism who wrote at the dawn of the nineteenth century were so entranced by the wide horizons which it opened before them, that they looked upon it as a new revelation, and upon themselves as upon the founders of a new religion. Socialism had to be a religion, and they had to regulate its march, as the heads of a new church. Besides, writing during the period of reaction which had followed the French Revolution, and seeing more its failures than its successes, they did not trust the masses, and they did not appeal to them for bringing about the changes which they thought necessary. They put their faith, on the contrary, into some great ruler. He would understand the new revelation ; he would be convinced of its desirability by the successful experiments of their phalansteries, or associations ; and he would peacefully accomplish by the means of his own authority the revolution which would bring well-being and happiness to manklnd. A military genius, Napoleon, had just been ruling Europe. . . . Why should not a social genius come forward and carry Europe with him and transfer the new Gospel into life ? . . . That faith was rooted very deep, and it stood for a long time in the way of Socialism ; its traces are ever seen amongst us, down to the present day.

It was only during the years 1840-48, when the approach of the Revolution was felt everywhere, and the proletarians were beginning to plant the banner of Socialism on the barricades, that faith in the people began to enter once more the hearts of the social schemers : faith, on the one side, in Republican Democracy, and on the other side in *free* association and the organizing powers of the working-men themselves.

But then came the Revolution of February, 1848, the middle-class Republic, and—with it, broken hopes. Four months only after the proclamation of the Republic, the June insurrection of the Paris proletarians broke out, and it was crushed in blood. The wholesale shooting of the workingmen, the mass deportations to New Guinea, and finally the Napoleonian *coup d'etat followed.* The Socialists were prosecuted with fury, and the weeding out was so terrible and so thorough that for the next twelve or fifteen years the very traces of Socialism disappeared ; its literature vanished so completely that even names, once so familiar before 1848, were entirely forgotten ; ideas which were then current—the stock ideas of the Socialists before 1848—were wiped out of the memories and were taken, later on, by the present generation, for new discoveries.

However, when a new revival came, about 1866, when Communism and Collectivism once more came forward, the conception as to the means of their realization had undergone a deep change. The old faith in Political Democracy was gone, and the first principles upon which the Paris working-men agreed with the British trade-unionists and Owenites, when they met in 1866 at London, was that " the emancipation of the working-men must be accomplished by the working- men themselves." Upon another point they also fell in. It was that the labour unions themselves would have to get hold of the instruments of production, and organize production themselves. The French idea of the Fourierist and Mutualist " Association " thus joined hands with Robert Owen's idea of " The Great Consolidated Trades' Union," which was extended now, so as to become an International Working-men's Association.

Again this new revival of Socialism lasted but a few years. Soon came the war of 1870-71, the uprising of the Paris Commune—and again the free development of Socialism was rendered impossible in France. But while Germany accepted now from the hands of its German teachers, Marx and Engels, the Socialism of the French " fortyeighters "—the Socialism of Considerant and Louis Blanc, and the Collectivism of Pecqueur,—France made a further step forward.

In March, 1871, Paris had proclaimed that henceforward it would not wait for the retardatory portions of France, and intended to start within its Commune its own social development.

The movement was too short-lived to give any positive result. It remained communalist only. But the working-classes of the old International saw at once its historical significance. They understood that the free commune would be henceforth the medium in which the ideas of modern Socialism may come to realization. The free agro-industrial communes, of which so much was spoken in 1848, need not be small phalansteries, or small communities of 2000 persons. They must be vast agglomerations, like Paris, or, still better, small territories. These communes would federate, even irrespectively of national frontiers (like the Cinque Ports, or the Hansa) ; and large labour associations might come into existence for the inter-communal service of the railways, the docks, and so on. Such were the ideas which began vaguely to circulate after 1871 amongst the thinking working-men, especially in the Latin countries. In some such organization, the details of which Ufe itself would settle, the labour circles of these countries saw the medium through which SociaUst forms of hfe could find a much easier reahzation than through the CoUectivist system of the State Sociahsts.

These are the ideas to which I have endeavoured to give a more or less definite expression in this book.

Looking back now at the years that have passed since this book was written, I can say in full conscience that its leading ideas must have been correct. The State Socialism of the collectivist system has certainly made some progress. State railways, State banking, and State trade in spirits have been introduced here and there. But every step made in this direction, even though it resulted in the cheapening of a given commodity, was found to be a new obstacle in the struggle of the working-men for their emancipation. So that we find now amongst the working-men, especially in this country, the idea that even the working of such a vast national property as a railway-net could be much better handled by a Federated Union of railway employes, than by a State organization.

On the other side, we see that countless attempts have been made all over Europe and America, the leading idea of which is, on the one side, to get into the hands of the working-men themselves wide branches of production, and, on the other side, to always widen in the cities the circles of the functions which the city performs in the interest of its inhabitants. Trade-unionism, with a growing tendency towards organizing the different trades internationally, and of being not only an instrument for improving the conditions of labour, but also to become an organization which might, at a given moment, take into its hands the management of production ; Co-operativism, both for production and for distribution, both in industry and agriculture, and attempts at combining both sorts of cooperation in experimental colonies ; and finally, the immensely varied field of the so-called Municipal Socialism—these are the three directions in which the greatest amount of creative power has been developed lately.

Of course, none of these may, in any degree, be taken as a substitute for Communism, or even for Sociahsm, both of which imply the common possession of the instruments of production. But we certainly must look at all the just-mentioned attempts as upon experiments—like those which Owen, Fourier, and Saint Simon tried in their colonies—experiments which prepare human thought to conceive some of the practical forms in which a communist society might find its expression. The synthesis of all these partial experiments will have to be made some day by the constructive genius of some one of the civilized nations, and it will be done. But samples of the bricks out of which the great synthetic building will have to be built, and even samples of some of its rooms, are being prepared by the immense effort of the constructive genius of man.

BROMLEY, KENT.

October, 1906.

CHAPTER-I

OUR RICHES

I

The human race has travelled far since, those bygone ages when men used to fashion their rude implements of flint, and lived on the precarious spoils of the chase, leaving to their children for their only heritage a shelter beneath the rocks, some poor utensils—and Nature, vast, ununderstood, and terrific, with whom they had to fight for their wretched existence.

During the agitated times which have elapsed since, and which have lasted for many thousand years, mankind has nevertheless amassed untold treasures. It has cleared the land, dried the marshes, pierced the forests, made roads; it has been building, inventing, observing, reasoning; it has created a complex machinery, wrested her secrets from Nature, and finally it has made a servant of steam. And the result is, that now the child of the civilized man finds ready, at its birth, to his hand an immense capital accumulated by those who have gone before him. And this capital enables him to acquire, merely by his own labour, combined with the labour of others, riches surpassing the dreams of the Orient, expressed in the fairy tales of the Thousand and One Nights.

The soil is cleared to a great extent, fit for the reception of the best seeds, ready to make a rich return for the skill and labour spent upon it— a return more than sufficient for all the wants of humanity. The methods of cultivation are known.

On the wide prairies of America each hundred men, with the aid of powerful machinery, can produce in a few months enough wheat to maintain ten thousand people for a whole year. And where man wishes to double his produce, to treble it, to multiply it a hundred-fold, he makes the soil, gives to each plant the requisite care, and thus obtains enormous returns. While the hunter of old had to scour fifty or sixty square miles to find food for his family, the civilized man supports his household, with far less pains, and far more certainty, on a thousandth part of that space. Climate is no longer an obstacle.

When the sun fails, man replaces it by artificial heat; and we see the coming of a time when artificial light also will be used to stimulate vegetation. Meanwhile, by the use of glass and hot water pipes, man renders a given space ten and fifty times more productive than it was in its natural state.

The prodigies accomplished in industry are still more striking. With the co-operation of those intelligent beings, modern machines—themselves the fruit of three or four generations of inventors, mostly unknown—a hundred men manufacture now the stuff to clothe ten thousand persons for a period of two years. In well-managed coal mines the labour of a hundred miners furnishes each year enough fuel to warm ten thousand families under an inclement sky. And we have lately witnessed twice the spectacle of a wonderful city springing up in a few months at Paris,1 without interrupting in the slightest degree the regular work of the French nation.

And if in manufactures as in agriculture, and as indeed through our whole social system, the labour, the discoveries, and the inventions of our ancestors profit chiefly the few, it is none the less certain that mankind in general, aided by the creatures of steel and iron which it already possesses, could already procure an existence of wealth and ease for every one of its members.

Truly, we are rich, far richer than we think; rich in what we already possess, richer still in the possibilities of production of our actual mechanical outfit; richest of all in what we might win from our soil, from our manufactures, from our science, from our technical knowledge, were they but applied to bringing about the well-being of all.

II

We, in civilized societies, are rich. Why then are the many poor? Why this painful drudgery for the masses? Why, even to the best paid workman, this uncertainty for the morrow, in the midst of all the wealth inherited from the past, and in spite of the powerful means of production, which could ensure comfort to all in return for a few hours of daily toil?

The Socialists have said it and repeated it unwearyingly. Daily they reiterate it, demonstrating it by arguments taken from all the sciences. It is because all that is necessary for production— the land, the mines, the highways, machinery, food, shelter, education, knowledge—all have been seized by the few in the course of that long story of robbery, enforced migration and wars, of ignorance and oppression, which has been the life of the human race before it had learned to subdue the forces of Nature. It is because, taking advantage of alleged rights acquired in the past, these few appropriate to-day two-thirds of the products of human labour, and then squander them in the most stupid and shameful way. It is because, having reduced the masses to a point at which they have not the means of subsistence for a month, or even for a week in advance, the few only allow the many to work on condition of themselves receiving the lion's share. It is because these few prevent the remainder of men from producing the things they need, and force them to produce, not the necessaries of life for all, but whatever offers the greatest profits to the monopolists. In this is the substance of all Socialism.

Take, indeed, a civilized country. The forests which once covered it have been cleared, the marshes drained, the climate improved. It has been made habitable. The soil, which bore formerly only a coarse vegetation, is covered to-day with rich harvests. The rock-walls in the valleys are laid out in terraces and covered with vines bearing golden fruit. The wild plants, which yielded nought but acrid berries, or uneatable roots, have been transformed by generations of culture into succulent vegetables, or trees covered with delicious fruits. Thousands of highways and railroads furrow the earth, and pierce the mountains. The shriek of the engine is heard in the wild gorges of the Alps, the Caucasus, and the Himalayas. The rivers have been made navigable; the coasts, carefully surveyed, are easy of access; art)ficial harbours, laboriously dug out and protected against the fury of the sea, afford shelter to the ships. Deep shafts have been sunk in the rocks; labyrinths of underground galleries have been dug out where coal may be raised or minerals extracted. At the crossings of the highways great cities have sprung up, and within their borders all the treasures of industry, science, and art have been accumulated.

Whole generations, that lived and died in misery, oppressed and ill-treated by their masters, and worn out by toil, have handed on this immense inheritance to our century.

For thousands of years millions of men have laboured to clear the forests, to drain the marshes, and to open up highways by land and water. Every rood of soil we cultivate in Europe has been watered by the sweat of several races of men. Every acre has its story of enforced labour, of intolerable toil, of the peoplc's sufferings. Every mile of railway, every yard of tunnel, has received its share of human blood.

The shafts of the mine still bear on their rocky walls the marks made by the pick of the workman who toiled to excavate them. The space between each prop in the underground galleries might be marked as a miner's grave; and who can tell what each of these graves has cost, in tears, in privations, in unspeakable wretchedness to the family who depended on the scanty wage of the worker cut off in his prime by fire-damp, rock-fall, or flood?

The cities, bound together by railroads and waterways, are organisms which have lived through centuries. Dig beneath them and you find, one above another, the foundations of streets, of houses, of theatres, of public buildings. Search into their history and you will see how the civilization of the town, its industry, its special characteristics, have slowly grown and ripened through the co-operation of generations of its inhabitants before it could become what it is to-day. And even to-day; the value of each dwelling, factory, and warehouse, which has been created by the accumulated labour of the millions of workers, now dead and buried, is only maintained by the very presence and labour of legions of the men who now inhabit that special corner of the globe. Each of the atoms composing what we call the Wealth of Nations owes its value to the fact that it is a part of the great whole. What would a London dockyard or a great Paris warehouse be if they were not situated in these great centres of international commerce? What would become of our mines, our factories, our workshops, and our railways, without the immense quantities of merchandise transported every day by sea and land?

Millions of human beings have laboured to create this civilization on which we pride ourselves to-day. Other millions, scattered through the globe, labour to maintain it. Without them nothing would be left in fifty years but ruins.

There is not even a thought, or an invention, which is not common property, born of the past and the present. Thousands of inventors, known and unknown, who have died in poverty, have co-operated in the invention of each of these machines which embody the genius of man.

Thousands of writers, of poets, of scholars, have laboured to increase knowledge, to dissipate error, and to create that atmosphere of scientific thought, without which the marvels of our century could never have appeared. And these thousands of philosophers, of poets, of scholars, of inventors, have themselves been supported by the labour of past centuries. They have been upheld and nourished through life, both physically and mentally, by legions of workers and craftsmen of all sorts. They have drawn their motive force from the environment.

The genius of a Séguin, a Mayer, a Grove, has certainly done more to launch industry in new directions than all the capitalists in the world. But men of genius are themselves the children of industry as well as of science. Not until thousands of steam-engines had been working for years before all eyes, constantly transforming heat into dynamic force, and this force into sound, light, and electricity, could the insight of genius proclaim the mechanical origin and the unity of the physical forces. And if we, children of the nineteenth century, have at last grasped this idea, if we know now how to apply it, it is again because daily experience has prepared the way. The thinkers of the eighteenth century saw and declared it, but the idea remained undeveloped, because the eighteenth century had not grown up like ours, side by side with the steam-engine. Imagine the decades that might have passed while we remained in ignorance of this law, which has revolutionized modern industry, had Watt not found at Soho skilled workmen to embody his ideas in metal, bringing all the parts of his engine to perfection, so that steam, pent in a complete mechanism, and rendered more docile than a horse, more manageable than water, became at last the very soul of modern industry.

Every machine has had the same history—a long record of sleepless nights and of poverty, of disillusions and of joys, of partial improvements discovered by several generations of nameless workers, who have added to the original invention these little nothings, without which the most fertile idea would remain fruitless. More than that: every new invention is a synthesis, the resultant of innumerable inventions which have preceded it in the vast field of mechanics and industry.

Science and industry, knowledge and application, discovery and practical realization leading to new discoveries, cunning of brain and of hand, toil of mind and muscle—all work together. Each discovery, each advance, each increase in the sum of human riches, owes its being to the physical and mental travail of the past and the present.

By what right then can any one whatever appropriate the least morsel of this immense whole and say—This is mine, not yours?

III

It has come about, however, in the course of the ages traversed by the human race, that all that enables man to produce, and to increase his power of production, has been seized by the few. Sometime, perhaps, we will relate how this came to pass. For the present let it suffice to state the fact and analyse its consequences.

To-day the soil, which actually owes its value to the needs of an ever-increasing population, belongs to a minority who prevent the people from cultivating it—or do not allow them to cultivate it according to modern methods.

The mines, though they represent the labour of several generations, and derive their sole value from the requirements of the industry of a nation and the density of the population—the mines also belong to the few; and these few restrict the output of coal, or prevent it entirely, if they find more profitable investments for their capital. Machinery, too, has become the exclusive property of the few, and even when a machine incontestably represents the improvements added to the original rough invention by three or four generations of workers, it none the less belongs to a few owners. And if the descendants of the very inventor who constructed the first machine for lace-making, a century ago, were to present themselves to-day in a lace factory at BÃ¢le or Nottingham, and demand their rights, they would be told: "Hands off! this machine is not yours," and they would be shot down if they attempted to take possession of it.

The railways, which would be useless as so much old iron without the teeming population of Europe, its industry, its commerce, and its marts, belong to a few shareholders, ignorant perhaps of the whereabouts of the lines of rails which yield them revenues greater than those of medieval kings. And if the children of those who perished by thousands while excavating the railway cuttings and tunnels were to assemble one day, crowding in their rags and hunger, to demand bread from the shareholders, they would be met with bayonets and grape-shot, to disperse them and safeguard "vested interests."

In virtue of this monstrous system, the son of the worker, on entering life, finds no field which he may till, no machine which he may tend, no mine in which he may dig, without accepting to leave a great part of what he will produce to a master. He must sell his labour for a scant and uncertain wage. His father and his grandfather have toiled to drain this field, to build this mill, to perfect this machine. They gave to the work the full measure of their strength, and what more could they give? But their heir comes into the world poorer than the lowest savage. If he obtains leave to till the fields, it is on condition of surrendering a quarter of the produce to his master, and another quarter to the government and the middlemen. And this tax, levied upon him by the State, the capitalist, the lord of the manor, and the middleman, is always increasing; it rarely leaves him the power to improve his system of culture. If he turns to industry, he is allowed to work—though not always even that —only on condition that he yield a half or two-thirds of the product to him whom the land recognizes as the owner of the machine.

We cry shame on the feudal baron who forbade the peasant to turn a clod of earth unless he surrendered to his lord a fourth of his crop. We call those the barbarous times. But if the forms have changed, the relations have remained the same, and the worker is forced, under the name of free contract, to accept feudal obligations. For, turn where he will, he can find no better conditions. Everything has become private property, and he must accept, or die of hunger.

The result of this state of things is that all our production tends in a wrong direction. Enterprise takes no thought for the needs of the community. Its only aim is to increase the gains of the speculator. Hence the constant fluctuations of trade, the periodical industrial crises, each of which throws scores of thousands of workers on the streets.

The working people cannot purchase with their wages the wealth which they have produced, and industry seeks foreign markets among the monied classes of other nations. In the East, in Africa, everywhere, in Egypt, Tonkin or the Congo, the European is thus bound to promote the growth of serfdom. And so he does. But soon he finds everywhere similar competitors. All the nations evolve on the same lines, and wars, perpetual wars, break out for the right of precedence in the market. Wars for the possession of the East, wars for the empire of the sea, wars to impose duties on imports and to dictate conditions to neighbouring states; wars against those "blacks" who revolt! The roar of the cannon never ceases in the world, whole races are massacred, the states of Europe spend a third of their budgets in armaments; and we know how heavily these taxes fall on the workers.

Education still remains the privilege of a small minority, for it is idle to talk of education when the workman's child is forced, at the age of thirteen, to go down into the mine or to help his father on the farm. It is idle to talk of studies to the worker, who comes home in the evening crushed by excessive toil with its brutalizing atmosphere. Society is thus bound to remain divided into two hostile camps, and in such conditions freedom is a vain word. The Radical begins by demanding a greater extension of political rights, but he soon sees that the breath of liberty leads to the uplifting of the proletariat, and then he turns round, changes his opinions, and reverts to repressive legislation and government by the sword.

A vast array of courts, judges, executioners, policemen, and gaolers is needed to uphold these privileges; and this array gives rise in its turn to a whole system of espionage, of false witness, of spies, of threats and corruption.

The system under which we live checks in its turn the growth of the social sentiment. We all know that without uprightness, without self-respect, without sympathy and mutual aid, human kind must perish, as perish the few races of animals living by rapine, or the slave-keeping ants. But such ideas are not to the taste of the ruling classes, and they have elaborated a whole system of pseudo-science to teach the contrary.

Fine sermons have been preached on the text that those who have should share with those who have not, but he who would act out this principle is speedily informed that these beautiful sentiments are all very well in poetry, but not in practice. "To lie is to degrade and besmirch oneself," we say, and yet all civilized life becomes one huge lie. We accustom ourselves and our children to hypocrisy, to the practice of a double-faced morality. And since the brain is ill at ease among lies, we cheat ourselves with sophistry. Hypocrisy and sophistry become the second nature of the civilized man.

But a society cannot live thus; it must return to truth or cease to exist.

Thus the consequences which spring from the original act of monopoly spread through the whole of social life. Under pain of death, human societies are forced to return to first principles: the means of production being the collective work of humanity, the product should be the collective property of the race. Individual appropriation is neither just nor serviceable. All belongs to all. All things are for all men, since all men have need of them, since all men have worked in the measure of their strength to produce them, and since it is not possible to evaluate every one's part in the production of the world's wealth.

All things are for all. Here is an immense stock of tools and implements; here are all those iron slaves which we call machines, which saw and plane, spin and weave for us, unmaking and remaking, working up raw matter to produce the marvels of our time. But nobody has the right to seize a single one of these machines and say, "This is mine; if you want to use it you must pay me a tax on each of your products," any more than the feudal lord of medieval times had the right to say to the peasant, "This hill, this meadow belong to me, and you must pay me a tax on every sheaf of corn you reap, on every rick you build."

All is for all! If the man and the woman bear their fair share of work, they have a right to their fair share of all that is produced by all, and that share is enough to secure them well-being. No more of such vague formulas as "The Right to work," or "To each the whole result of his labour." What we proclaim is THE RIGHT TO WELL-BEING: WELL-BEING FOR ALL!

CHAPTER-II

WELL-BEING FOR ALL

I

Well-being for all is not a dream. It is possible, realizable, owing to all that our ancestors have done to increase our powers of production.

We know, indeed, that the producers, although they constitute hardly one-third of the inhabitants of civilized countries, even now produce such quantities of goods that a certain degree of comfort could be brought to every hearth. We know further that if all those who squander to-day the fruits of others' toil were forced to employ their leisure in useful work, our wealth would increase in proportion to the number of producers, and more. Finally, we know that contrary to the theory enunciated by Malthus—that Oracle of middle-class Economics —the productive powers of the human race increase at a much more rapid ratio than its powers of reproduction. The more thickly men are crowded on the soil, the more rapid is the growth of their wealth-creating power.

Thus, although the population of England has only increased from 1844 to 1890 by 62 per cent, its production has grown, to say the least, at double that rate—to wit, by 130 per cent. In France, where the population has grown more slowly, the increase in production is nevertheless very rapid. Notwithstanding the crises through which agriculture is frequently passing, notwithstanding State interference, the blood-tax (conscription), and speculative commerce and finance, the production of wheat in France has increased fourfold, and industrial production more than tenfold, in the course of the last eighty years. In the United States the progress is still more striking. In spite of immigration, or rather precisely because of the influx of surplus European labour, the United States have multiplied their wealth tenfold.

However, these figures give yet a very faint idea of what our wealth might become under better conditions. For alongside of the rapid development of our wealth-producing powers we have an overwhelming increase in the ranks of the idlers and middlemen. Instead of capital gradually concentrating itself in a few hands, so that it would only be necessary for the community to dispossess a few millionaires and enter upon its lawful heritage— instead of this Socialist forecast proving true, the exact reverse is coming to pass: the swarm of parasites is ever increasing.

In France there are not ten actual producers to every thirty inhabitants. The whole agricultural wealth of the country is the work of less than seven millions of men, and in the two great industries, mining and the textile trade, you will find that the workers number less than two and one-half millions. But the exploiters of labour, how many are they?— In England (exclusive of Scotland and Ireland), only one million workers—men, women, and children—are employed in all the textile trades, rather more than half a million work the mines, rather less than half a million till the ground, and the statisticians have to exaggerate all the figures in order to establish a maximum of eight million producers to twenty-six million inhabitants. Strictly speaking the creators of the goods exported from Britain to all the ends of the earth comprise only from six to seven million workers. And what is the sum of the shareholders and middlemen who levy the first fruits of labour from far and near, and heap up unearned gains by thrusting themselves between the producer and the consumer, paying the former not a fifth, nay, not a twentieth, of the price they exact from the latter?

Nor is this all. Those who withhold capital constantly reduce the output by restraining production. We need not speak of the cartloads of oysters thrown into the sea to prevent a dainty, hitherto reserved for the rich, from becoming a food for the people. We need not speak of the thousand and one luxuries — stuffs, foods, etc. etc.—treated after the same fashion as the oysters. It is enough to remember the way in which the production of the most necessary things is limited. Legions of miners are ready and willing to dig out coal every day, and send it to those who are shivering with cold; but too often a third, or even two-thirds, of their number are forbidden to work more than three days a week, because, forsooth, the price of coal must be kept up? Thousands of weavers are forbidden to work the looms, though their wives and children go in rags, and though three-quarters of the population of Europe have no clothing worthy the name.

Hundreds of blast-furnaces, thousands of factories oeriodically stand idle, others only work half-time —and in every civilized nation there is a permanent population of about two million individuals who ask only for work, but to whom work is denied.

How gladly would these millions of men set to work to reclaim waste lands, or to transform illcultivated land into fertile fields, rich in harvests! A year of well-directed toil would suffice to multiply fivefold the produce of dry lands in the south of France which now yield only about eight bushels of wheat per acre. But these men, who would be happy to become hardy pioneers in so many branches of wealth-producing activity, must stay their hands because the owners of the soil, the mines, and the factories prefer to invest their capital—stolen in the first place from the community—in Turkish or Egyptian bonds, or in Patagonian gold mines, and so make Egyptian fellahs, Italian exiles, and Chinese coolies their wage-slaves.

So much for the direct and deliberate limitation of production; but there is also a limiltation indirect and not of set purpose, which consists in spending human toil on objects absolutely useless, or destined only to satisfy the dull vanity of the rich.

It is impossible to reckon in figures the extent to which wealth is restricted indirectly, the extent to which energy is squandered, that might have served to produce, and above all to prepare the machinery necessary to production. It is enough to cite the immense sums spent by Europe in armaments for the sole purpose of acquiring control of the markets, and so forcing her own commercial standards on neighbouring territories and making exploitation easier at home; the millions paid every year to officials of all sorts, whose function it is to maintain the rights of minorities—the right, that is, of a few rich men—to manipulate the economic activities of the nation; the millions spent on judges, prisons, policemen, and all the paraphernalia of so-called justice—spent to no purpose, because we know that every alleviation, however slight, of the wretchedness of our great cities is followed by a very considerable diminution of crime; lastly, the millions spent on propagating pernicious doctrines by means of the press, and news "cooked" in the interest of this or that party, of this politician or of that company of exploiters.

But over and above this we must take into account all the labour that goes to sheer waste, in keeping up the stables, the kennels, and the retinue of the rich, for instance; in pandering to the caprices of society and to the depraved tastes of the fashionable mob; in forcing the consumer on the one hand to buy what he does not need, or foisting an inferior article upon him by means of puffery, and in producing on the other hand wares which are absolutely injurious, but profitable to the manufacturer. What is squandered in this manner would be enough to double our real wealth, or so to plenish our mills and factories with machinery that they would soon flood the shops with all that is now lacking to two-thirds of the nation. Under our present system a full quarter of the producers in every nation are forced to be idle for three or four months in the year, and the labour of another quarter, if not of the half, has no better results than the amusement of the rich or the exploitation of the public.

Thus, if we consider on the one hand the rapidity with which civilized nations augment their powers of production, and on the other hand the limits set to that production, be it directly or indirectly, by existing conditions, one cannot but conclude that an economic system a trifle more enlightened would permit them to heap up in a few years so many useful products that they would be constrained to cry—"Enough! We have enough coal and bread and raiment ! Let us rest and consider how best to use our powers, how best to employ our leisure."

No, plenty for all is not a dream—though it was a dream indeed in those old days when man, for all his pains, could hardly win a bushel of wheat from an acre of land, and had to fashion by hand all the implements he used in agriculture and industry. Now it is no longer a dream, because man has invented a motor which, with a little iron and a few pounds of coal, gives him the mastery of a creature strong and docile as a horse, and capable of setting the most complicated machinery in motion.

But, if plenty for all is to become a reality, this immense capital—cities, houses, pastures, arable lands, factories, highways, education—must cease to be regarded as private property, for the monopolist to dispose of at his pleasure.

This rich endowment, painfully won, builded, fashioned, or invented by our ancestors, must become common property, so that the collective interests of men may gain from it the greatest good for all.

There must be EXPROPRIATION. The well-being of all—the end; expropriation—the means.

II

Expropriation, such then is the problem which History has put before the men of the twentieth century: the return to Communism in all that ministers to the well-being of man.

But this problem cannot be solved by means of egislation. No one imagines that. The poor, no less than the rich, understand that neither the existing Governments, nor any which might arise out of possible political changes, would be capable of finding a solution. We feel the necessity of a social revolution; rich and poor alike recognize that this revolution is imminent, that it may break out in a very few years.

A great change in thought has been accomplished during the last half of the nineteenth century; but suppressed, as it was, by the propertied classes, and denied its natural development, this new spirit must break now its bonds by violence and realize itself in a revolution.

Whence comes the revolution, and how will it announce its coming? None can answer these questions. The future is hidden. But those who watch and think do not misinterpret the signs: workers and exploiters, Revolutionists and Conservatives, thinkers and men of action, all feel that the revolution is at our doors.

Well! What are we to do when the thunderbolt has fallen?

We have all been studying the dramatic side of revolution so much, and the practical work of revolution so little, that we are apt to see only the stage effects, so to speak, of these great movements; the fight of the first days; the barricades. But this fight, this first skirmish, is soon ended, and it is only after the overthrow of the old constitution that the real work of revolution can be said to begin.

Effete and powerless, attacked on all sides, the old rulers are soon swept away by the breath of insurrection. In a few days the middle-class monarchy of 1848 was no more, and while Louis Philippe was making good his escape in a cab, Paris had already forgotten her "citizen king." The government of Thiers disappeared, on the I8th of March, I871, in a few hours, leaving Paris mistress of her destinies. Yet 1848 and I871 were only insurrections. Before a popular revolution the masters of "the old order" disappear with a surprising rapidity. Its upholders fly the country, to plot in safety elsewhere and to devise measures for their return.

The former Government having disappeared, the army, hesitating before the tide of popular opinion, no longer obeys its commanders, who have also prudently decamped. The troops stand by without interfering, or join the rebels. The police, standing at ease, are uncertain whether to belabour the crowd or to cry: "Long live the Commune!" while some retire to their quarters "to await the pleasure of the new Government." Wealthy citizens pack their trunks and betake themselves to places of safety. The people remain. This is how a revolution is ushered in. In several large towns the Commune is proclaimed. In the streets wander thousands of men, who in the evening crowd into improvised clubs asking: "What shall we do?" and ardently discuss public affairs, in which all take an interest; those who yesterday were most indifferent are perhaps the most zealous. Everywhere there is plenty of goodwill and a keen desire to make victory certain. It is a time of supreme devotion. The people are ready to go forward.

All this is splendid, sublime; but still, it is not a revolution. Nay, it is only now that-the work of the revolutionist begins.

Doubtless the thirst for vengeance will be satisfied. The Watrins and the Thomases will pay the penalty of their unpopularity, but that is only an incident of the struggle and not a revolution.

Socialist politicians, radicals, neglected geniuses of journalism, stump orators, middle-class citizens, and workmen hurry to the Town Hall to the Government offices, and take possession of the vacant seats. Some rejoice their hearts with galloon, admire themselves in ministerial mirrors, and study to give orders with an air of importance appropriate to their new position. They must have a red sash, an embroidered cap, and magisterial gestures to impress their comrades of the office or the workshop! Others bury themselves in official papers, trying, with the best of wills, to make head or tail of them. They indite laws and issue high-flown worded decrees that nobody takes the trouble to carry out— because the revolution has come. To give themselves an authority which is lacking they seek the sanction of old forms of Government. They take the names of "Provisional Government," "Committee of Public Safety," "Mayor," "Governor of the Town Hall," " Commissioner of Public Weal," and what not. Elected or acclaimed, they assemble in Boards or in Communal Councils. These bodies include men of ten or twenty different schools, which, if not exactly "private chapels," are at least so many sects which represent as many ways of regarding the scope, the bearing, and the goal of the revolution. Possibilists, Collectivists, Radicals, Jacobins, Blanquists, are thrust together, and waste time in wordy warfare. Honest men come into contact with ambitious ones, whose only dream is power and who spurn the crowd whence they sprung. Coming together with diametrically opposed views, they are forced to form arbitrary alliances in order to create majorities that can but last a day. Wrangling, calling each other reactionaries, authoritarians, and rascals, incapable of coming to an understanding on any serious measure, dragged into discussions about trifles, producing nothing better than bombastic proclamations, yet taking themselves seriously, unwitting that the real strength of the movement is in the streets.

All this may please those who like the theatre, but it is not revolution. Nothing yet has been accomplished Meanwhile the people suffer. The factories are idle, the workshops closed; industry is at a standstill. The worker does not even earn the meagre wage which was his before. Food goes up in price. With that heroic devotion which has always characterized them, and which in great crises reaches the sublime, the people wait patiently. "We place these three months of want at the service of the Republic," they said in 1848, while "their representatives" and the gentlemen of the new Government, down to the meanest Jack-in-office, received their salary regularly.

The people suffer. With the childlike faith, with the good humour of the masses who believe in their leaders, they think that "yonder," in the House, in the Town Hall, in the Committee of Public Safety, their welfare is being considered. But "yonder" they are discussing everything under the sun except the welfare of the people. In 1793, while famine ravaged France and crippled the Revolution; whilst the people were reduced to the depths of misery, whilst the Champs Ã‰lysée were lined with luxurious carriages where women displayed their jewels and splendour, Robespierre was urging the Jacobins to discuss his treatise on the English Constitution. While the worker was suffering in 1848 from the general stoppage of trade the Provisional Government and the House were wrangling over military pensions and prison labour, without troubling how the people were to live during this crisis. And could one cast a reproach at the Paris Commune, which was born beneath the Prussian cannon, and lasted only seventy days, it would be for this same error— this failure to understand that the Revolution could not triumph unless those who fought on its side were fed, that on fifteen pence a day a man cannot fight on the ramparts and at the same time support a family.

The people suffer and say: "How to find the way out of these difficulties?"

III

It seems to us that there is only one answer to this question: We must recognize, and loudly proclaim, that every one, whatever his grade in the old society, whether strong or weak, capable or incapable, has, before everything, THE RIGHT TO LIVE, and that society is bound to share amongst all, without exception, the means of existence at its disposal. We must acknowledge this, and proclaim it aloud, and act up to it.

It must be so contrived that from the first day of the revolution the worker shall know that a new era is opening before him; that henceforward none need crouch under the bridges, with palaces hard by, none need fast in the midst of food, none need perish with cold near shops full of furs; that all is for all, in practice as well as in theory, and that at last, for the first time in history, a revolution has been accomplished which considers the NEEDS of the people before schooling them in their DUTIES.

This cannot be brought about by Acts of Parlia- meet, but only by taking immediate and effective possession of all that is necessary to ensure the well-being of all; this is the only really scientific way of going to work, the only way to be understood and desired by the mass of the people. We must take possession, in the name of the people, of the granaries, the shops full of clothing, and the dwelling houses. Nothing must be wasted. We must organize without delay to feed the hungry, to satisfy all wants, to meet all needs, to produce, not for the special benefit of this one or that one, but to ensure that society as a whole will live and grow.

Enough of ambiguous words like "the right to work," with which the people were misled in 1848, and which are still used to mislead them. Let us have the courage to recognize that *Well-being for all*, henceforward possible, must be realized.

When the workers claimed the right to work in 1848, national and municipal workshops were organized, and workmen were sent to drudge there at the rate of 1s. 8d. a day! When they asked that labour should be organized, the reply was: "Patience, friends, the Government will see to it; meantime here is your 1s. 8d. Rest now, brave toiler, after your lifelong struggle for food!" Meantime the cannons were trained, the reserves called out, and the workers themselves disorganized by the many methods well known to the middle classes, till one fine day they were told to go and colonize Africa or be shot down.

Very different will be the result if the workers claim the right to well-being! In claiming that right they claim the right to possess the wealth of the community—to take the houses to dwell in, according to the needs of each family; to seize the stores of food and learn the meaning of plenty, after having known famine too well. They proclaim their right to all wealth—fruit of the labour of past and present generations—and learn by its means to enjoy those higher pleasures of art and science too long monopolized by the middle classes.

And while asserting their right to live in comfort, they assert, what is still more important, their right to decide for themselves what this comfort shall be, what must be produced to ensure it, and what discarded as no longer of value.

The "right to well-being" means the possibility of living like human beings, and of bringing up children to be members of a society better than ours, whilst the "right to work" only means the right to be always a wage-slave, a drudge, ruled over and exploited by the middle class of the future. The right to well-being is the Social Revolution, the right to work means nothing but the Treadmill of Commercialism. It is high time for the worker to assert his right to the common inheritance and to enter into possession.

CHAPTER-III

ANARCHIST COMMUNISM

I

Every society which has abolished private property will be forced, we maintain, to organize itself on the lines of Communistic Anarchy. Anarchy leads to Communism, and Communism to Anarchy, both alike being expressions of the predominant tendency in modern societies, the pursuit of equality.

Time was when a peasant family could consider the corn which it grew, or the woollen garments woven in the cottage, as the products of its own toil. But even then this way of looking at things was not quite correct. There were the roads and the bridges made in common, the swamps drained by common toil, and the communal pastures enclosed by hedges which were kept in repair by each and all. If the looms for weaving or the dyes for colouring fabrics were improved, all profited; so even in those days a peasant family could not live alone, but was dependent in a thousand ways on the village or the commune.

But nowadays, in the present state of industry, when everything is interdependent, when each branch of production is knit up with all the rest, the attempt to claim an Individualist origin for the products of industry is absolutely untenable. The astonishing perfection attained by the textile or mining industries in civilized countries is due to the simultaneous development of a thousand other industries, great and small, to the extension of the railroad system, to inter-oceanic navigation, to the manual skill of thousands of workers, to a certain standard of culture reached by the working classes as a whole, to the labours, in short, of men in every corner of the globe.

The Italians who died of cholera while making the Suez Canal, or of anchylosis in the St. Gothard Tunnel, and the Americans mowed down by shot and shell while fighting for the abolition of slavery have helped to develop the cotton industry in France and England, as well as the work-girls who languish in the factories of Manchester and Rouen, and the inventor who (following the suggestion of some worker) succeeds in improving the looms.

How, then, shall we estimate the share of each in the riches which ALL contribute to amass?

Looking at production from this general, synthetic point of view, we cannot hold with the Collectivists that payment proportionate to the hours of labour rendered by each would be an ideal arrangement, or even a step in the right direction.

Without discussing whether exchange value of goods is really measured in existing societies by the amount of work necessary to produce it—according to the doctrine of Smith and Ricardo, in whose footsteps Marx has followed—suffice it to say here, leaving ourselves free to return to the subject later, that the Collectivist ideal appears to us untenable in a society which considers the instruments of labour as a common inheritance. Starting from this principle, such a society would find itself forced from the very outset to abandon all forms of wages.

The mitigated individualism of the collectivist system certainly could not maintain itself alongside a partial communism—the socialization of land and the instruments of production. A new form of property requires a new form of remuneration. A new method of production cannot exist side by side with the old forms of consumption, any more than it can adapt itself to the old forms of political organization.

The wage system arises out of the individual ownership of the land and the instruments of labour. It was the necessary condition for the development of capitalist production, and will perish with it, in spite of the attempt to disguise it as "profit-sharing." The common possession of the instruments of labour must necessarily bring with it the enjoyment in common of the fruits of common labour.

We hold further that Communism is not only desirable, but that existing societies, founded on Individualism, *are inevitably impelled in the direction of Communism.* The development of Individualism during the last three centuries is explained by the efforts of the individual to protect himself from the tyranny of Capital and of the State. For a time he imagined, and those who expressed his thought for him declared, that he could free himself entirely from the State and from society. "By means of money," he said, " I can buy all that I need." But the individual was on a wrong tack, and modern history has taught him to recognize that, without the help of all, he can do nothing, although his strong-boxes are full of gold.

In fact, alongside this current of Individualism, we find in all modern history a tendency, on the one hand, to retain all that remains of the partial Communism of antiquity, and, on the other, to establish the Communist principle in the thousand developments of modern life.

As soon as the communes of the tenth, eleventh, and twelfth centuries had succeeded in emancipating themselves from their lords, ecclesiastical or lay, their communal labour and communal consumption began to extend and develop rapidly. The township—and not private persons—freighted ships and equipped expeditions, and the benefit arising from the foreign trade did not accrue to individuals, but was shared by all. The townships also bought provisions for their citizens. Traces of these institutions have lingered on into the nineteenth century, and the folk piously cherish the memory of them in their legends.

All that has disappeared. But the rural township still struggles to preserve the last traces of this Communism, and it succeeds—except when the State throws its heavy sword into the balance.

Meanwhile new organizations, based on the same principle——*to every man according to his needs*— spring up under a thousand different forms; for without a certain leaven of Communism the present societies could not exist. In spite of the narrowly egoistic turn given to men's minds by the commercial system, the tendency towards Communism is constantly appearing, and influences our activities in a variety of ways

The bridges, for the use of which a toll was levied in the old days, are now become public property and free to all; so are the high roads, except in the East, where a toll is still exacted from the traveller for every mile of his journey. Museums, free libraries, free schools, free meals for children; parks and gardens open to all; streets paved and lighted, free to all; water supplied to every house without measure or stint—all such arrangements are founded on the principle: "Take what you need."

The tramways and railways have already introduced monthly and annual season tickets, without limiting the number of journeys taken; and two nations, Hungary and Russia, have introduced on their railways the zone system, which permits the holder to travel five hundred or a thousand miles for the same price. It is but a short step from that to a uniform charge, such as already prevails in the postal service. In all these innovations, and a thousand others, the tendency is not to measure the individual consumption. One man wants to travel a thousand miles, another five hundred. These are personal requirements. There is no sufficient reason why one should pay twice as much as the other because his need is twice as great. Such are the signs which appear even now in our individualist societies.

Moreover, there is a tendency, though still a feeble one, to consider the needs of the individual, irrespective of his past or possible services to the community. We are beginning to think of society as a whole, each part of which is so intimately bound up with the others that a service rendered to one is a service rendered to all.

When you go into a public library—not indeed the National Library of Paris, but, say, into the British Museum or the Berlin Library—the librarian does not ask what services you have rendered to society before giving you the book, or the fifty books which you require, and he comes to your assistance if you do not know how to manage the catalogue. By means of uniform credentials—and very often a contribution of work is preferred—the scientific society opens its museums, its gardens, its library, its laboratories, and its annual conversaziones to each of its members, whether he be a Darwin, or a simple amateur.

At St. Petersburg, if you are pursuing an invention, you go into a special laboratory or a workshop, where you are given a place, a carpenter's bench, a turning lathe, all the necessary tools and scientific instruments, provided only you know how to use them; and you are allowed to work there as long as you please. There are the tools; interest others in your idea, join with fellow workers skilled in various crafts, or work alone if you prefer it. Invent a flying machine, or invent nothing—that is your own affair. You are pursuing an idea—that is enough.

In the same way, those who man the lifeboat do not ask credentials from the crew of a sinking ship; they launch their boat, risk their lives in the raging waves, and sometimes perish, all to save men whom they do not even know. And what need to know them? "They are human beings, and they need our aid—that is enough, that establishes their right——To the rescue! "

Thus we find a tendency, eminently communistic, springing up on all sides, and in various guises, in the very heart of theoretically individualist societies.

Suppose that one of our great cities, so egotistic in ordinary times, were visited to-morrow by some calamity—a siege, for instance—that same selfish city would decide that the first needs to satisfy were those of the children and the aged. Without asking what services they had rendered, or were likely to render to society, it would first of all feed them. Then the combatants would be cared for, irrespective of the courage or the intelligence which each has displayed, and thousands of men and women would outvie each other in unselfish devotion to the wounded.

This tendency exists and is felt as soon as the most pressing needs of each are satisfied, and in proportion as the productive power of the race increases. It becomes an active force every time a great idea comes to oust the mean preoccupations of everyday life.

How can we doubt, then, that when the instruments of production are placed at the service of all, when business is conducted on Communist principles, when labour, having recovered its place of honour in society, produces much more than is necessary to all—how can we doubt but that this force (already so powerful) will enlarge its sphere of action till it becomes the ruling principle of social life?

Following these indications, and considering further the practical side of expropriation, of which we shall speak in the following chapters, we are convinced that our first obligation, when the revolution shall have broken the power upholding the present system, will be to realize Communism without delay.

But ours is neither the Communism of Fourier and the Phalansteriens, nor of the German State-Socialists. It is Anarchist Communism,—Communism without government—the Communism of the Free. It is the synthesis of the two ideals pursued by humamty throughout the ages— Economic and Political Liberty.

II

In taking "Anarchy" for our ideal of political organization we are only giving expression to another marked tendency of human progress. Whenever European societies have developed up to a certain point they have shaken off the yoke of authority and substituted a system founded roughly more or less on the principles of individual liberty. And history shows us that these periods of partial or general revolution, when the governments were overthrown, were also periods of sudden progress both in the economic and the intellectual field. Now it is the enfranchisement of the communes, whose monuments, produced by the free labour of the guilds, have never been surpassed; now it is the peasant rising which brought about the Reformation and imperilled the papacy; and then again it is the society, free for a brief space, which was created at the other side of the Atlantic by the malcontents from the Old World.

Further, if we observe the present development of civilized peoples we see, most unmistakably, a movement ever more and more marked to limit the sphere of action of the Government, and to allow more and more liberty to the individual. This evolution is going on before our eyes, though cumbered by the ruins and rubbish of old institutions and old superstitions. Like all evolutions, it only waits a revolution to overthrow the old obstacles which block the way, that it may find free scope in a regenerated society.

After having striven long in vain to solve the insoluble problem—the problem of constructing a government "which will constrain the individual to obedience without itself ceasing to be the servant of society," men at last attempt to free themselves from every form of government and to satisfy their need for organization by a free contract between individuals and groups pursuing the same aim. The independence of each small territorial unit becomes a pressing need; mutual agreement replaces law, and everywhere regulates individual interests in view of a common object.

All that was once looked on as a function of the Government is to-day called in question. Things are arranged more easily and more satisfactorily without the intervention of the State. And in studying the progress made in this direction, we are led to conclude that the tendency of the human race is to reduce Government interference to zero; in fact, to abolish the State, the personification of injustice, oppression, and monopoly.

We can already catch glimpses of a world in which the bonds which bind the individual are no longer laws, but social habits—the result of the need felt by each one of us to seek the support, the co-operation, the sympathy of his neighbours.

Assuredly the idea of a society without a State will give rise to at least as many objections as the political economy of a society without private capital. We have all been brought up from our childhood to regard the State as a sort of Providence; all our education, the Roman history we learned at school, the Byzantine code which we studied later under the name of Roman law, and the various sciences taught at the universities, accustom us to believe in Government and in the virtues of the State providential.

To maintain this superstition whole systems of philosophy have been elaborated and taught; all politics are based on this principle; and each politician, whatever his colours, comes forward and says to the people, "Give me the power, and I both can and will free you from the miseries which press so heavily upon you."

From the cradle to the grave all our actions are guided by this principle. Open any book on sociology or jurisprudence, and you will find there the Government, its organization, its acts, filling so large a place that we come to believe that there is nothing outside the Government and the world of statesmen.

The press teaches us the same in every conceivable way. Whole columns are devoted to parliamentary debates and to political intrigues. The vast every day life of a nation is barely mentioned in a few lines when dealing with economic subjects, law, or in "divers facts" relating to police cases. And when you read these newspapers, you hardly think of the incalculable number of beings—all humanity, so to say—who grow up and die, who know sorrow, who work and consume, think and create outside the few encumbering personages who have been so magnified that humanity is hidden by their shadows enlarged by our ignorance.

And yet as soon as we pass from printed matter; to life itself, as soon as we throw a glance at society, we are struck by the infinitesimal part played by the Government. Balzac already remarked how millions of peasants spend the whole of their lives without knowing anything about the State, save the heavy taxes they are compelled to pay. Every day millions of transactions are made without Government intervention, and the greatest of them— those of commerce and of the Exchange—are carried on in such a way that the Government could not be appealed to if one of the contracting parties had the intention of not furfilling his agreement. Should you speak to a man who understands commerce he will tell you that the everyday business transacted by merchants would be absolutely impossible were it not based on mutual confidence. The habit of keeping his word, the desire not to lose his credit, amply suffice to maintain this relative honesty. The man who does not feel the slightest remorse when poisoning his customers with noxious drugs covered with pompous labels thinks he is in honour bound to keep his engagements. Now, if this relative morality has developed under present conditions, when enrichment is the only incentive and the only aim, can we doubt its rapid progress when appropriation of the fruits of others' labour will no longer be the basis of society?

Another striking fact, which especially characterizes our generation, speaks still more in favour of our ideas. It is the continual extension of the field of enterprise due to private initiative, and the prodigious development of free groups of all kinds. We shall discuss this more at length in the chapter devoted to Free Agreement. Suffice it to mention that the facts are so numerous and so customary that they are the essence of the second half of the nineteenth century, even though political and socialist writers ignore them, always preferring to talk to us about the functions of Government.

These organizations, free and infinitely varied, are so natural an outcome of our civilization; they expand so rapidly and group themselves with so much ease; they are so necessary a result of the continual growth of the needs of civilized man; and lastly, they so advantageously replace governmental interference that we must recognize in them a factor of growing importance in the life of societies. If they do not yet spread over the whole of the manifestations of life, it is that they find an insurmountable obstacle in the poverty of the worker, in the casts of present society, in the private appropriation of capital, and in the State. Abolish these obstacles and you will see them covering the immense field of civilized man's activity.

The history of the last fifty years furnishes a living proof that Representative Government is impotent to discharge the functions we have sought to assign to it. In days to come the nineteenth century will be quoted as having witnessed the failure of parliamentarianism.

But this impotence is becoming evident to all; the faults of parliamentarianism, and the inherent vices of the representative principle, are self-evident, and the few thinkers who have made a critical study of them (J. S. Mill and Leverdays) did but give literary form to the popular dissatisfaction. It is not difficult, indeed, to see the absurdity of naming a few men and saying to them, "Make laws regulating all our spheres of activity, although not one of you knows anything about them!"

We are beginning to see that government by majorities means abandoning all the affairs of the country to the tide-waiters who make up the majorities in the House and in election committees; to those, in a word, who have no opinion of their own. But mankind is seeking and already finding new issues.

The International Postal Union, the railway unions, and the learned societies give us examples of solutions based on free agreement in place and stead of law.

To-day, when groups scattered far and wide wish to organize themselves for some object or other, they no longer elect an international parliament of Jacks-of-all-trades. No, where it is not possible to meet directly or come to an agreement by correspondence, delegates versed in the question at issue are sent to treat, with the instructions: "Endeavour to come to an agreement on such or such a question and then return not with a law in your pocket, but with a proposition of agreement which we may or may not accept."

Such is the method of the great industrial companies, the learned societies, and the associations of every description, which already cover Europe and the United States. And such should be the method of an emancipated society. While bringing about expropriation, society cannot continue to organize itself on the principle of parliamentary representation. A society founded on serfdom is in keeping with absolute monarchy; a society based on the wage system and the exploitation of the masses by the capitalists finds its political expression in parliamentarianism. But a free society, regaining possession of the common inheritance, must seek, in free groups and free federations of groups, a new organization, in harmony with the new economic phase of history.

Every economic phase has a political phase corresponding to it, and it would be impossible to touch property without finding at the same time a new mode of political life.

CHAPTER-IV

EXPROPRIATION

I

It is told of Rothschild that, seeing his fortune threatened by the Revolution of 1848, he hit upon the following stratagem: "I am quite willing to admit," said he, "that my fortune has been accumulated at the expense of others, but if it were divided to-morrow among the millions of Europe, the share of each would only amount to five shillings. Very well, then, I undertake to render to each his five shillings if he asks me for it."

Having given due publicity to his promise, our millionaire proceeded as usual to stroll quietly through the streets of Frankfort. Three or four passers-by asked for their five shillings, which he disbursed with a sardonic smile. His stratagem succeeded, and the family of the millionaire is still in possession of its wealth.

It is in much the same fashion that the shrewd heads among the middle classes reason when they say, "Ah, Expropriation! I know what that means. You take all the overcoats and lay them in a heap, and every one is free to help himself and fight for the best."

But such jests are irrelevant as well as flippant. What we want is not a redistribution of overcoats, although it must be said that even in such a case, the shivering folk would see advantage in it. Nor do we want to divide up the wealth of the Rothschilds. What we do want is so to arrange things that every human being born into the world shall be ensured the opportunity in the first instance of learning some useful occupation, and of becoming skilled in it; next, that he shall be free to work at his trade without asking leave of master or owner, and without handing over to landlord or capitalist the lion's share of what he produces. As to the wealth held by the Rothschilds or the Vanderbilts, it will serve us to organize our system of communal production.

The day when the labourer may till the ground without paying away half of what he produces, the day when the machines necessary to prepare the soil for rich harvests are at the free disposal of the cultivators, the day when the worker in the factory produces for the community and not the monopolist—that day will see the workers clothed and fed, and there will be no more Rothschilds or other exploiters.

No one will then have to sell his working power for a wage that only represents a fraction of what he produces.

"So far so good," say our critics, "but you will have Rothschilds coming in from outside. How are you to prevent a person from amassing millions in China and then settling amongst you? How are you going to prevent such a one from surrounding himself with lackeys and wage-slaves—from exploiting them and enriching himself at their expense?

"You cannot bring about a revolution all over the world at the same time. Well, then, are you going to establish custom-houses on your frontiers to search all who enter your country and confiscate the money they bring with them?—Anarchist policemen firing on travellers would be a fine spectacle!"

But at the root of this argument there is a great error. Those who propound it have never paused to inquire whence come the fortunes of the rich. A little thought would, however, suffice to show them that these fortunes have their beginnings in the poverty of the poor. When there are no longer any destitute there will no longer be any rich to exploit them.

Let us glance for a moment at the Middle Ages, when great fortunes began to spring up.

A feudal baron seizes on a fertile valley. But as long as the fertile valley is empty of folk our baron is not rich. His land brings him in nothing; he might as well possess a property in the moon.

What does our baron do to enrich himself? He looks out for peasants—for poor peasants!

If every peasant-farmer had a piece of land, free from rent and taxes, if he had in addition the tools and the stock necessary for farm labour, who would plough the lands of the baron? Everyone would look after his own. But there are thousands of destitute persons ruined by wars, or drought, or pestilence. They have neither horse nor plough. (Iron was costly in the Middle Ages, and a draughthorse still more so.)

All these destitute creatures are trying to better their condition. One day they see on the road at the confines of our baron's estate a notice-board indicating by certain signs adapted to their comprehension that the labourer who is willing to settle on this estate will receive the tools and materials to build his cottage and sow his fields, and a portion of land rent free for a certain number of years. The number of years is represented by so many crosses on the sign-board, and the peasant understands the meaning of these crosses.

So the poor wretches swarm over the baron's lands, making roads, draining marshes, building villages. In nine years he begins to tax them. Five years later he increases the rent. Then he doubles it. The peasant accepts these new conditions because he cannot find better ones elsewhere; and little by little, with the aid of laws made by the barons, the poverty of the peasant becomes the source of the landlord's wealth. And it is not only the lord of the manor who preys upon him. A whole host of usurers swoop down upon the villages, multiplying as the wretchedness of the peasants increases. That is how things went in the Middle Ages. And to-day is it not still the same thing? If there were free lands which the peasant could cultivate if he pleased, would he pay £50 to some "shabble of a duke"* for condescending to sell him a scrap? Would he burden himself with a lease which absorbed a third of the produce? Would he—on the *métayer* system—consent to give the half of his harvest to the landowner?

But he has nothing. So he will accept any conditions, if only he can keep body and soul together, while he tills the soil and enriches the landlord.

So in the nineteenth century, just as in the Middle Ages, the poverty of the peasant is a source of wealth to the landed proprietor.

II

The landlord owes his riches to the poverty of the peasants, and the wealth of the capitalist comes from the same source.

Take the case of a citizen of the middle class, who somehow or other finds himself in possession of £20,000. H could, of course, spend his money at the rate of £2,000 a year, a mere bagatelle in these days of fantastic, senseless luxury. But then he would have nothing left at the end of ten years. So, being a "practical person," he prefers to keep his fortune intact, and win for himself a snug little annual income as well.

This is very easy in our society, for the good reason that the towns and villages swarm with workers who have not the wherewithal to live for a month, or even a fortnight. So our worthy citizen starts a factory. The banks hasten to lend him another £20,000, especially if he has a reputation for "business ability"; and with this round sum he can command the labour of five hundred hands.

If all the men and women in the country-side had their daily bread sure and their daily needs already satisfied, who would work for our capitalist at a wage of half a crown a day, while the commodities one produces in a day sell in the market for a crown or more?

* "Shabble of a Duke" is an expression coined by Carlyle; it is a somewhat free rendering of Kropotkine's "Monsieur le Vicomte," but I think it expresses his meaning. — Trans.

Unhappily—we know it all too well—the poor quarters of our towns and the neighbouring villages are full of needy wretches, whose children clamour for bread. So, before the factory is well finished, the workers hasten to offer themselves. Where a hundred are required three hundred besiege the doors, and from the time his mill is started the owner, if he only has average business capacities, will clear £40 a year out of each mill-hand he employs.

He is thus able to lay by a snug little fortune; and if he chooses a lucrative trade and has "business talents" he will soon increase his income by doubling the number of the men he exploits.

So he becomes a personage of importance. He can afford to give dinners to others personages—to the local magnates, the civic, legal, and political dignitaries. With his money he can "marry money"; by and by he may pick and choose places for his children, and later on perhaps get something good from the Government—a contract for the army or for the police. His gold breeds gold; till at last a war, or even a rumour of war, or a speculation on the Stock Exchange, gives him his great opportunity.

Nine-tenths of the great fortunes made in the United States are (as Henry George has shown in this "Social Problems") the result of knavery on a large scale, assisted by the State. In Europe, nine-tenths of the fortunes made in our monarchies and republics have the same origin. There are not two ways of becoming a millionaire.

This is the secret of wealth; find the starving and destitute, pay them half a crown, and make them produce five shillings worth in the day, amass a fortune by these means, and then increase it by some lucky hit, made with the help of the State.

Need we go on to speak of small fortunes attributed by the economists to forethought and frugality, when we know that mere saving in itself brings in nothing, so long as the pence saved are not used to exploit the famishing?

Take a shoemaker, for instance. Grant that his work is well paid, that he has plenty of custom, and that by dint of strict frugality he contrives to lay by from eighteen pence to two shillings a day, perhaps two pounds a month.

Grant that our shoemaker is never ill, that he does not half starve himself, in spite of his passion for economy; that he does not marry or that he has no children; that he does not die of consumption; suppose anything and everything you please!

Well, at the age of fifty he will not have scraped together £800; and he will not have enough to live on during his old age, when he is past work. Assuredly this is not how great fortunes are made. But suppose our shoemaker, as soon as he has laid by a few pence, thriftily conveys them to the savings bank, and that the savings bank lends them to the capitalist who is just about to "employ labour," i.e. to exploit the poor. Then our shoemaker takes an apprentice, the child of some poor wretch, who will think himself lucky if in five years time his son has learned the trade and is able to earn his living.

Meanwhile our shoemaker does not lose by him, and if trade is brisk he soon takes a second, and then a third apprentice. By and by he will take two or three working men—poor wretches, thankful to receive half a crown a day for work that is worth five shillings, and if our shoemaker is "in luck," that is to say, if he is keen enough and mean enough, his working men and apprentices will bring him in nearly one pound a day, over and above the product of his own toil. He can then enlarge his business. He will gradually become rich, and no longer have any need to stint himself in the necessaries of life. He will leave a snug little fortune to his son.

That is what people call "being economical and having frugal, temperate habits." At bottom it is nothing more nor less than grinding the face of the poor.

Commerce seems an exception to this rule. "Such a man," we are told, "buys tea in China, brings it to France, and realizes a profit of thirty per cent on his original outlay. He has exploited nobody."

Nevertheless the case is analogous. If our merchant had carried his bales on his back, well and good! In early medieval times that was exactly how foreign trade was conducted, and so no one reached such giddy heights of fortune as in our days. Very few and very hardly earned were the gold coins which the medieval merchant gained from a long and dangerous voyage. It was less the love of money than the thirst of travel and adventure that inspired his undertakings.

Nowadays the method is simpler. A merchant who has some capital need not stir from his desk to become wealthy. He telegraphs to an agent telling him to buy a hundred tons of tea; he freights a ship, and in a few weeks, in three months if it is a sailing ship, the vessel brings him his cargo. He does not even take the risks of the voyage, for his tea and his vessel are insured, and if he has expended four thousand pounds he will receive more than five thousand; that is to say, if he has not attempted to speculate in some novel commodities, in which case he runs a chance of either doubling his fortune or losing it altogether.

Now, how could he find men willing to cross the sea, to travel to China and back, to endure hardship and slavish toil and to risk their lives for a miserable pittance? How could he find dock labourers willing to load and unload his ships for "starvation wages"? How? Because they are needy and starving. Go to the seaports, visit the cook-shops and taverns on the quays, and look at these men who have come to hire themselves, crowding round the dock-gates, which they besiege from early dawn, hoping to be allowed to work on the vessels. Look at these sailors, happy to be hired for a long voyage, after weeks and months of waiting. All their lives long they have gone to the sea in ships, and they will sail in others still, until they have perished in the waves.

Enter their homes, look at their wives and children in rags, living one knows not how till the father's return, and you will have the answer to the question. Multiply examples, choose them where you will, consider the origin of all fortunes, large or small, whether arising out of commerce, finance, manufactures, or the land. Everywhere you will find that the wealth of the wealthy springs from the poverty of the poor. This is why an anarchist society need not fear the advent of a Rothschild who would settle in its midst. If every member of the community knows that after a few hours of productive toil he will have a right to all the pleasures that civilization procures, and to those deeper sources of enjoyment which art and science offer to all who seek them, he will not sell his strength for a starvation wage. No one will volunteer to work for the enrichment of your Rothschild. His golden guineas will be only so many pieces of metal—useful for various purposes, but incapable of breeding more.

In answering the above objection we have at the same time indicated the scope of Expropriation. It must apply to everything that enables any man—be he financier, mill-owner, or landlord—to appropriate the product of others' toil. Our formula is simple and comprehensive.

We do not want to rob any one of his coat, but we wish to give to the workers all those things the lack of which makes them fall an easy prey to the exploiter, and we will do our utmost that none shall lack aught, that not a single man shall be forced to sell the strength of his right arm to obtain a bare subsistence for himself and his babes. This is what we mean when we talk of Expropriation; this will be our duty during the Revolution, for whose coming we look, not two hundred years hence, but soon, very soon.

III

The ideas of Anarchism in general and of Expropriation in particular find much more sympathy than we are apt to imagine among men of independent character, and those for whom idleness is not the supreme ideal. "Still," our friends often warn us, "take care you do not go too far! Humanity cannot be changed in a day, so do not be in too great a hurry with your schemes of Expropriation and Anarchy, or you will be in danger of achieving no permanent result."

Now, what we fear with regard to Expropriation is exactly the contrary. We are afraid of not going far enough, of carrying out Expropriation on too small a scale to be lasting. We would not have the revolutionary impulse arrested in mid-career, to exhaust itself in half measures, which would content no one, and while producing a tremendous confusion in society, and stopping its customary activities, would have no vital power—would merely spread general discontent and inevitably prepare the way for the triumph of reaction.

There are, in fact, in a modern State established relations which it is practically impossible to modify if one attacks them only in detail. There are wheels within wheels in our economic organization—the machinery is so complex and interdependent that no one part can be modified without disturbing the whole. This becomes clear as soon as an attempt is made to expropriate anything.

Let us suppose that in a certain country a limited form of expropriation is effected. For example, that, as it has been suggested more than once, only the property of the great landlords is socialized, whilst the factories are left untouched; or that, in a certain city, house property is taken over by the Commune, but everything else is left in private ownership; or that, in some manufacturing centre, the factories are communalized, but the land is not interfered with.

The same result would follow in each case—a terrible shattering of the industrial system, without the means of reorganizing it on new lines. Industry and finance would be at a deadlock, yet a return to the first principles of justice would not have been achieved, and society would find itself powerless to construct a harmonious whole.

If agriculture could free itself from great landowners, while industry still remained the bondslave of the capitalist, the merchant, and the banker, nothing would be accomplished. The peasant suffers to-day not only in having to pay rent to the landlord; he is oppressed on all hands by existing conditions. He is exploited by the tradesman, who makes him pay half a crown for a spade which, measured by tile labour spent on it, is not worth more than sixpence. He is taxed by the State, which cannot do without its formidable hierarchy of officials, and finds it necessary to maintain an expensive army, because the traders of all nations are perpetually fighting for the markets, and any day a little quarrel arising from the exploitation of some part of Asia or Africa may result in war.

Then again the peasant suffers from the depopulation of country places: the young people are attracted to the large manufacturing towns by the bait of high wages paid temporarily by the producers of articles of luxury, or by the attractions of a more stirring life. The artificial protection of industry, the industrial exploitation of foreign countries, the prevalence of stock-jobbing, the difficulty of improving the soil and the machinery of production—all these agencies combine nowadays to work against agriculture, which is burdened not only by rent, but by the whole complex of conditions in a society based on exploitation. Thus, even if the expropriation of land were accomplished, and every one were free to till the soil and cultivate it to the best advantage, without paying rent, agriculture, even though it should enjoy—which can by no means be taken for granted—a momentary prosperity, would soon into the slough in which it finds itself to-day. The whole thing would have to be begun over again, with increased difficulties.

The same holds true of industry. Take the converse case: instead of turning the agricultural labourers into peasant-proprietors, make over the factories to those who work in them. Abolish the master-manufacturers, but leave the landlord his land, the banker his money, the merchant his Exchange, maintain the swarm of idlers who live on the toil of the workmen, the thousand and one middlemen, the State with its numberless officials, and industry would come to a standstill. Finding no purchasers in the mass of peasants who would remain poor; not possessing the raw material, and unable to export their produce, partly on account of the stoppage of trade, and still more so because industries spread all over the world, the manufacturers would feel unable to struggle, and thousands of workers would be thrown upon the streets. These starving crowds would be ready and willing to submit to the first schemer who came to exploit them; they would even consent to return to the old slavery, if only under promise of work.

Or, finally, suppose you oust the landowners, and hand over the mills and factories to the worker, without interfering with the swarm of middlemen who drain the product of our manufacturers, and speculate in corn and flour, meat and groceries, in our great centres of commerce. Then, as soon as exchange is arrested, the great cities are left without bread, and others find no buyers for their articles of luxury, a terrible counter-revolution will take place—a counter-revolution treading upon the slain, sweeping the towns and villages with shot and shell; there would be proscriptions, panic, flight, tend all the terrors of the guillotine, as it was in France in 1815, 1848, and 1871.

All is interdependent in a civilized society; it is impossible to reform any one thing without altering the whole. Therefore, on the day we strike at private property, under any one of its forms, territorial or industrial, we shall be obliged to attack them all. The very success of the Revolution will demand it.

Besides, we could not, if we would, confine ourselves to a partial expropriation. Once the principle of the "Divine Right of Property" is shaken, no amount of theorizing will prevent its overthrow, here by the slaves of the toil, there by the slaves of the machine.

If a great town, Paris for example, were to confine itself to taking possession of the dwelling houses or the factories, it would be forced also to deny the right of the bankers to levy upon the Commune a tax amounting to £2,000,000 in the form of interest for former loans. The great city would be obliged to put itself in touch with the rural districts, and its influence would inevitably urge the peasants to free themselves from the landowner. It would be necessary to communalize the railways, that the citizens might get food and work, and lastly, to prevent the waste of supplies, and to guard against the trust of corn-speculators, like those to whom the Commune of 1793 fell a prey, it would have to place in the hands of the City the work of stocking its warehouses with commodites, and apportioning the produce.

Nevertheless, some Socialists still seek to establish a distinction. "Of course," they say, "the soil, the mines, the mills, and manufactures must be expropriated, these are the instruments of production, and it is right we should consider them public property. But articles of consumption—food, clothes, and dwellings—should remain private property."

Popular common sense has got the better of this subtle distinction. We are not savages who can live in the woods, without other shelter than the branches. The civilized man needs a roof, a room, a hearth, and a bed. It is true that the bed, the room, and the house is a home of idleness for the non-producer. But for the worker, a room, properly heated and lighted, is as much an instrument of production as the tool or the machine. It is the place where the nerves and sinews gather strength for the work of the morrow. The rest of the workman is the daily repairing of the machine.

The same argument applies even more obviously to food. The so-called economists of whom we speak would hardly deny that the coal burnt in a machine is as necessary to production as the raw material itself. How then can food, without which the human machine could do no work, be excluded from the list of things indispensable to the producer? Can this be a relic of religious metaphysics? The rich man's feast is indeed a matter of luxury, but the food of the worker is just as much a part of production as the fuel burnt by the steam-engine.

The same with clothing. If the economists who draw this distinction between articles of production and of consumption dressed themselves in the fashion of New Guinea, we could understand their objection. But men who could not write a word without a shirt on their back are not in a position to draw such a hard and fast line between their shirt and their pen. And though the dainty gowns of their dames must certainly rank as objects of luxury, there is nevertheless a certain quantity of linen, cotton, and woollen stuff which is a necessity of life to the producer. The shirt and shoes in which he goes to his work, his cap and the jacket he slips on after the day's toil is over, these are as necessary to him as the hammer to the anvil.

Whether we like it or not, this is what the people mean by a revolution. As soon as they have made a clean sweep of the Government, they will seek first of all to ensure to themselves decent dwellings and sufficient food and clothes—free of capitalist rent.

And the people will be right. The methods of the people will be much more in accordance with science than those of the economists who draw so many distinctions between instruments of production and articles of consumption. The people understand that this is just the point where the Revolution ought to begin; and they will lay the foundations of the only economic science worthy the name—a science which might be called *"The Study of the Needs of Humanity, and of the Economic Means to satisfy them."*

CHAPTER-V

FOOD

I

If the coming Revolution is to be a Social Revolution it will be distinguished from all former uprisings not only by its aim, but also by its methods. To attain a new end, new means are required.

The three great popular movements which we have seen in France during the last hundred years differ from each other in many ways, but they have one common feature.

In each case the people strove to overturn the old regime, and spent their heart's blood for the cause. Then, after having borne the brunt of the battle, they sank again into obscurity. A Government, composed of men more or less honest, was formed and undertook to organize—the Republic in 1793, Labour in 1848, and the Free Commune in 1871. Imbued with Jacobin ideas, this Government occupied itself first of all with political questions, such as the reorganization of the machinery of government, the purifying of the administration, the separation of Church and State, civic liberty, and such matters. It is true the workmen's clubs kept an eye on the members of the new Government, and often imposed their ideas on them. But even in these clubs, whether the leaders belonged to the middle or to the working classes, it was always middle-class ideas which prevailed. They discussed various political questions at great length, but forgot to discuss the question of bread.

Great ideas sprang up at such times, ideas that have moved the world; words were spoken which still stir our hearts, at the interval of a century. But the people were starving in the slums.

From the very commencement of the Revolution industry inevitably came to a stop—the circulation of produce was checked, and capital concealed itself. The master—the employer—had nothing to fear at such times, he battened on his dividends, if indeed he did not speculate on the wretchedness around; but the wage-earner was reduced to live from hand to mouth. Want knocked at the door.

Famine was abroad in the land—such famine as had hardly been seen under the old regime.

"The Girondists are starving us!" was the cry in the workmen's quarters in 1793, and thereupon the Girondists were guillotined, and full powers were given to "the Mountain" and to the Commune. The Commune indeed concerned itself with the question of bread, and made heroic efforts to feed Paris. At Lyons, Fouché and Collot d'Herbois established city granaries, but the sums spent on fillmg them were woefully insuffcient. The town councils made great efforts to procure corn; the bakers who hoarded flour were hanged—and still the people lacked bread.

Then they turned on the royalist conspirators and laid the blame at their door. They guillotined a dozen or fifteen a day—servants and duchesses alike, especially servants, for the duchesses had gone to Coblentz. But if they had guillotined a hundred dukes and viscounts every day, it would have been equally hopeless.

The want only grew. For the wage-earner can not live without his wage, and the wage was not forthcoming. What difference could a thousand corpses more or less make to him?

Then the people began to grow weary. "So much for your vaunted Revolution! You are more wretched than ever before," whispered the reactionary in the ears of the worker. And little by little the rich took courage, emerged from their hiding-places, and flaunted their luxury in the face of the starving multitude. They dressed up like scented fops and said to the workers: "Come, enough of this foolery! What have you gained by rebellion ?"

Sick at heart, his patience at an end, the revolutionary had at last to admit to himself that the cause was lost once more. He retreated into his hovel and awaited the worst.

Then reaction proudly asserted itself, and accomplished a politic stroke. The Revolution dead, nothing remained but to trample its corpse under foot.

The White Terror began. Blood flowed like water, the guillotine was never idle, the prisons were crowded, while the pageant of rank and fashion resumed its olcl course, and went on as merrily as before.

This picture is typical of all our revolutions. In 1848 the workers of Paris placed "three months of starvation" at the service of the Republic, and then, having reached the limit of their powers, they made one last desperate effort—an effort which was drowned in blood. In 1871 the Commune perished for lack of combatants. It had taken measures for the separation of Church and State, but it neglected, alas, until too late, to take measures for providing the people with bread. And so it came to pass in Paris that *élégantes* and fine gentlemen could spurn the confederates, and bid them go sell their lives for a miserable pittance, and leave their "betters" to feast at their ease in fashionable restaurants.

At last the Commune saw its mistake, and opened communal kitchens. But it was too late. Its days were already numbered, and the troops of Versailles were on the ramparts.

"Bread, it is bread that the Revolution needs!"

Let others spend their time in issuing pompous proclamations, in decorating themselves lavishly with official gold lace, and in talking about political liberty!...

Be it ours to see, from the first day of the Revolution to the last, in all the provinces fighting for freedom, that there is not a single man who lacks bread, not a single woman compelled to stand with the weariful crowd outside the bake-house-door, that haply a coarse loaf may be thrown to her in charity, not a single child pining for want of food.

It has always been the middle-class idea to harangue about "great principles"—great lies rather!

The idea of the people will be to provide bread for all. And while middle-class citizens, and workmen infested with middle-class ideas admire their own rhetoric in the "Talking Shops," and "practical people" are engaged in endless discussions on forms of government, we, the "Utopian dreamers"—we shall have to consider the question of daily bread.

We have the temerity to declare that all have a right to bread, that there is bread enough for all, and that with this watchword of Bread for All the Revolution will triumph.

II

That we are Utopians is well known. So Utopian are we that we go the length of believing that the Revolution can and ought to assure shelter, food, and clothes to all—an idea extremely displeasing to middle-class citizens, whatever their party colour, for they are quite alive to the fact that it is not easy to keep the upper hand of a people whose hunger is satisfied.

All the same, we maintain our contention: bread must be found for the people of the Revolution, and the question of bread must take precedence of all other questions. If it is settled in the interests of the people, the Revolution will be on the right road; for in solving the question of Bread we must accept the principle of equality, which will force itself upon us to the exclusion of every other solution.

It is certain that the coming Revolution—like in that respect to the Revolution of 1848—will burst upon us in the middle of a great industrial crisis. Things have been seething for half a century now, and can only go from bad to worse. Everything tends that way—new nations entering the, lists of international trade and fighting for possession of the world's markets, wars, taxes ever increasing. National debts, the insecurity of the morrow, and huge colonial undertakings in every corner of the globe.

There are millions of unemployed workers in Europe at this moment. It will be still worse when Revolution has burst upon us and spread like fire laid to a train of gunpowder. The number of the out-of-works will be doubled as soon as barricades are erected in Europe and the United States. What is to be done to provide these multitudes with bread?

We do not know whether the folk who call them selves "practical people" have ever asked themselves this question in all its nakedness. But we do know that they wish to maintain the wage system, and we must therefore expect to have "national workshops" and "public works" vaunted as a means of giving food to the unemployed.

Because national workshops were opened in 1789 and in 1793; because the same means were resorted to in 1848; because Napoleon III succeeded in contenting the Parisian proletariat for eighteen years by giving them public works—which cost Paris to-day its debt of £80,000,000—and its municipal tax of three or four pounds a-head;* because this excellent method of "taming the beast" was customary in Rome, and even in Egypt four thousand years ago; and lastly, because despots, kings, and emperors have always employed the ruse of throwing a scrap of food to the people to gain time to snatch up the whip—it is natural that "practical" men should extol this method of perpetuating the wage system. What need to rack our brains when we have the time-honoured method of the Pharaohs at our disposal?

Yet should the Revolution be so misguided as to start on this path, it would be lost.

In 1848, when the national workshops were opened on February 27, the unemployed of Paris numbered only 800; a fortnight later they had already increased to 49,000. They would soon have been 100,000, without counting those who crowded in from the provinces.

Yet at that time trade and manufacturers in France only employed half as many hands as to-day. And we know that in time of Revolution exchange and industry suffer most from the general upheaval.

To realize this we have only to think for a moment of the number of workmen whose labour depends directly or indirectly upon export trade, or of the number of hands employed in producing luxuries, whose consumers are the middle-class minority.

---

* The mnnicipal debt of Paris amounted 101904to2,266,S79,ioo francs, and the charges for it were 121,000,000 francs.

A revolution in Europe means the unavoidable stoppage of at least half the factories and workshops. It means millions of workers and their families thrown on the streets.

And our "practical men" would seek to avert this truly terrible situation by means of national relief works; that is to say, by means of new industries created on the spot to give work to the unemployed!

It is evident, as Proudhon has already pointed out, that the smallest attack upon property will bring in its train the complete disorganization of the system based upon private enterprise and wage labour. Society itself will be forced to take production in hand, in its entirety, and to reorganize it to meet the needs of the whole people. But this cannot be accomplished in a day or a month; it must take a certain time thus to reorganize the system of production, and during this time millions of men will be deprived of the means of subsistence. What then is to be done ?

There is only one really practical solution of the problem—boldly to face the great task which awaits us, and instead of trying to patch up a situation which we ourselves have made untenable, to proceed to reorganize production on a new basis.

Thus the really practical course of action, in our view, would be that the people should take immediate possession of all the food of the insurgent districts, keeping strict account of it all, that none might be wasted, and that by the aid of these accumulated resources every one might be able to tide over the crisis. During that time an agreement would have to be made with the factory workers, the necessary raw material given them and the means of subsistence assured to them while they worked to supply the needs of the agriculture population. For we must not forget that while France weaves silks and satins to deck the wives of German financiers, the Empress of Russia, and the Queen of the Sandwich Islands, and while Paris fashions wonderful trinkets and playthings for rich folk all the world over, two-thirds of the French peasantry have not proper lamps to give them light, or the implements necessary for modern agriculture. Lastly, unproductive land, of which there is plenty, would have to be turned to the best advantage, poor soils enriched, and rich soils, which yet, under the present system, do not yield a quarter, no, nor a tenth of what they might produce, submitted to intensive culture and tilled with as much care as a market garden or a flower plot. It is impossible to imagine any other practical solution of the problem; and, whether we like it or not, sheer force of circumstances will bring it to pass.

III

The most prominent characteristic of capitalism is the wage system, which in brief amounts to this:—

A man, or a group of men, possessing the necessary capital, starts some industrial enterprise; he undertakes to supply the factory or workshops with raw material, to organize production, to pay the employés a fixed wage, and lastly, to pocket the surplus value or profits, under pretext of recouping himself for managing the concern, for running the risks it may involve, and for the fluctuations of price in the market value of the wares.

To preserve this system, those who now monopolize capital would be ready to make certain concessions; to share, for example, a part of the profits with the workers, or rather to establish a "sliding scale," which would oblige them to raise wages when prices were high; in brief, they would consent to certain sacrifices on condition that they were still allowed to direct industry and to take its first fruits.

Collectivism, as we know, does not abolish wages, though it introduces considerable modifications into the existing order of things. It only substitutes the State, that is to say, Representative Government, national or local, for the individual employer of labour. Under Collectivism it is the representatives of the nation, or of the district, and their deputies and officials who are to have the control of industry. It is they who reserve to themselves the right of employing the surplus of; production—in the interests of all. Moreover, Collectivism draws a very subtle but very far reaching distinction between the work of the labourer and of the man who has learned a craft. Unskilled labour in the eyes of the collectivist is simple labour, while the work of the craftsman, the mechanic, the engineer, the man of science, etc., is what Marx calls complex labour, and is entitled to a higher wage. But labourers and craftsmen, weavers and men of science, are all wage-servants of the State—"all officials," as was said lately, to gild the pill.

The coming Revolution can render no greater service to humanity than to make the wage system, in all its forms, an impossibility, and to render Communism, which is the negation of wage-slavery, the only possible solution.

For even admitting that the Collectivist modification of the present system is possible, if introduced gradually during a period of prosperity and peace—though for my part I question its practicability even under such conditions—it would become impossible in a period of Revolution, when the need of feeding hungry millions springs up with the first call to arms. A political revolution can be accomplished without shaking the foundations of industry, but a revolution where the people lay hands upon property will inevitably paralyse exchange and production. Millions of public money would not suffice for wages to the millions of out-of-works.

This point cannot be too much insisted upon; the reorganization of industry on a new basis (and we shall presently show how tremendous this problem is) cannot be accomplished in a few days, nor, on the other hand, will the people submit to be half starved for years in order to oblige the theorists who uphold the wage system. To tide over the period of stress they will demand what they have always demanded in such cases—communization of supplies—the giving of rations.

It will be in vain to preach patience. The people will be patient no longer, and if food is not put in common they will plunder the bakeries.

If the people are not strong enough to carry all before them, they will be shot down to give Collectivism a fair field for experiment. To this end "order" must be maintained at any price—order, discipline, obedience! And as the capitalists will soon realize that when the people are shot down by those who call themselves Revolutionists, the Revolution itself will become hateful in the eyes of the masses; they will certainly lend their support to the champions of order—even though they are collectivists. In such a line of conduct, the capitalists will see a means of hereafter crushing the collectivists in their turn. If "order is established" in this fashion, the consequences are easy to foresee. Not content with shooting down the "marauders," the faction of "order" will search out the "ringleaders of the mob." They will set up again the law courts and reinstate the hangman. The most ardent revolutionists will be sent to the scaffold. It will be 1793 over again.

Do not let us forget how reaction triumphed in the last century. First the "Hébertists," "the madmen," were guillotined—those whom Mignet, with the memory of the struggle fresh upon him, still called " Anarchists." The Dantonists soon followed them; and when the party of Robespierre had guillotined these revolutionaries, they in their turn had to mount the scaffold; whereupon the people, sick of bloodshed, and seeing the revolution lost, threw up the sponge, and let the reactionaries do their worst.

If "order is restored," we say, the social democrats will hang the anarchists; the Fabians will hang the social democrats, and will in their turn be hanged by the reactionaries; and the Revolution will come to an end.

But everything confirms us in the belief that the energy of the people will carry them far enough, and that, when the Revolution takes place, the idea of anarchist Communism will have gained ground. It is not an artificial idea. The people themselves have breathed it in our ear, and the number of communists is ever increasing, as the impossibility of any other solution becomes more and more evident.

And if the impetus of the people is strong enough, affairs will take a very different turn. Instead of plundering the bakers' shops one day, and starving the next, the people of the insurgent cities will take possession of the warehouses, the cattle markets,—in fact of all the provision stores and of all the food to be had. The well-intentioned citizens, men and women both, will form themselves into bands of volunteers and address themselves to the task of making a rough general inventory of the contents, of each shop and warehouse. In twenty-four hours the revolted town or district will know what Paris has not found out yet, in spite of its statistical committees, and what it never did find out during the siege—the quantity of provisions it contains. In forty-eight hours millions of copies will be printed of the tables giving a sufficiently exact account of the available food, the places where it is stored, and the means of distribution.

In every block of houses, in every street, in every town ward, bands of volunteers will have been organized. These commissariat volunteers will work in unison and keep in touch with each other. If only the Jacobin bayonets do not get in the way; if only the self-styled "scientific" theorists do not thrust themselves in to darken counsel! Or rather let then expound their muddle-headed theories as much as they like, provided they have no authority, no power! And that admirable spirit of organization inherent in the people, above all in every social grade of the French nation,* but which they have so seldom been allowed to exercise, will initiate, even in so huge a city as Paris, and in the midst of a Revolution, an immense guild of free workers, ready to furnish to each and all the necessary food.

Give the people a free hand, and in ten days the food service will be conducted with admirable regularity. Only those who have never seen the people hard at work, only those who have passed their lives buried among documents, can doubt it. Speak of the organizing genius of the "Great Misunderstood," the people, to those who have seen it in Paris in the days of the barricades, or in London during the great dockers strike, when half a million of starving folk had to be fed, and they will tell you how superior it is to the official ineptness of Bumbledom.

And even supposing we had to endure a certain amount of discomfort and confusion for a fortnight or a month, surely that would not matter very much. For the mass of the people it would still be an improvement on their former condition; and, besides, in times of Revolution one can dine contentedly enough on a bit of bread and cheese while eagerly discussing events.

In any case, a system which springs up spontaneously, under stress of immediate need, will be infinitely preferable to anything invented between four walls by hide-bound theorists sitting on any number of committees.

IV

The people of the great towns will be driven by force of circumstances to take possession of all the provisions, beginning with the barest necessaries,

* Kropotkine is here supposing the Revolution to break out first in France.— Trans.

and gradually extending Communism to other things, in order to satisfy the needs of all the citizens.

The sooner it is done the better; the sooner it is done the less misery there will be and the less strife.

But upon what basis must society be organized in order that all may share and share alike? This is the question that meets us at the outset.

We answer that there are no two ways of it. There is only one way in which Communism can be established equitably, only one way which satisfies our instincts of justice and is at the same time practical, namely, the system already adopted by the agrarian communes of Europe.

Take for example a peasant commune, no matter where, even in France, where the Jacobins have, done their best to destroy all communal usage. If the commune possesses woods and copses, then, so long as there is plenty of wood for all, every one can take as much as he wants, without other let or hindrance than the public opinion of his neighbours. As to the timber-trees, which are always scarce, they have to be carefully apportioned.

The same with the communal pasture land; while there is enough and to spare, no limit is put to what the cattle of each homestead may consume, nor to the number of beasts grazing upon the pastures. Grazing grounds are not divided, nor is fodder doled out, unless there is scarcity. All the Swiss communes, and many of those in France and Germany too, wherever there is communal pasture land, practice this system.

And in the countries of Eastern Europe, where there are great forests and no scarcity of land, you find the peasants felling the trees as they need them, and cultivating as much of the soil as they require, without any thought of limiting each man's share of timber or of land. But the timber will be divided, and the land parcelled out, to each household according to its needs, as soon as either becomes scarce, as is already the case in Russia.

In a word, the system is this: no stint or limit to what the community possesses in abundance, but equal sharing and dividing of those commodities which are scarce or apt to run short. Of the three hundred and fifty millions who inhabit Europe, two hundred millions still follow this system of natural Communism.

It is a fact worth remarking that the same system prevails in the great towns in the distribution of one commodity at least, which is found in abundance, the water supplied to each house.

As long as there is no fear of the supply running short, no water company thinks of checking the consumption of water in each house. Take what you please! But during the great droughts, if there is any fear of supply failing, the water companies know that all they have to do is to make known the fact, by means of a short advertisement in the papers, and the citizens will reduce their consumption of water and not let it run to waste.

But if water were actually scarce, what would be done? Recourse would be had to a system of rations. Such a measure is so natural, so inherent in common sense, that Paris twice asked to be put on rations during the two sieges which it underwent in 1871.

Is it necessary to go into details, to prepare tables showing how the distribution of rations may work, to prove that it is just and equitable, infinitely more just and equitable than the existing state of things? All these tables and details will not serve to convince those of the middle classes, nor, alas, those of the workers tainted with middle-class prejudices, who regard the people as a mob of savages ready to fall upon and devour each other, directly the Government ceases to direct affairs. But those only who have never seen the people resolve and act on their own initiative could doubt for a moment that if the masses were masters of the situation, they would distribute rations to each and all in strictest accordance with justice and equity.

If you were to give utterance, in any gathering of people, to the opinion that delicacies—game and such-like—should be reserved for the fastidious palates of aristocratic idlers, and black bread given to the sick in the hospitals, you would be hissed. But say at the same gathering, preach at the street corners and in the market places, that the most tempting delicacies ought to be kept for the sick and feeble—especially for the sick. Say that if there are only five brace of partridge in the entire city, and only one case of sherry wine, they should go to sick people and convalescents. Say that after the sick come the children. For them the milk of the cows and goats should be reserved if there is not enough for all. To the children and the aged the last piece of meat, and to the strong man dry bread, if the community be reduced to that extremity.

Say, in a word, that if this or that article of consumption runs short, and has to be doled out, to those who have most need most should be given. Say that and see if you do not meet with universal agreement.

The man who is full-fed does not understand this, but the people do understand, have always understood it; and even the child of luxury, if he is thrown on the street and comes into contact with the masses, even he will learn to understand.

The theorists—for whom the soldier's uniform and the barrack mess table are civilization's last word—would like no doubt to start a regime of National Kitchens and "Spartan Broth." They would point out the advantages thereby gained, the economy in fuel and food, if such huge kitchens were established, where every one could come for their rations of soup and bread and vegetables.

We do not question these advantages. We are well aware that important economies have already been achieved in this direction—as, for instance, when the handmill, or quern, and the baker's oven attached to each house were abandoned. We can see perfectly well that it would be more economical to cook broth for a hundred families at once, instead of lighting a hundred separate fires. We know, besides, that there are a thousand ways of doing up potatoes, but that cooked in one huge pot for a hundred families they would be just as good.

We know, in fact, that variety in cooking being a matter of the seasoning introduced by each cook or housewife, the cooking together of a hundred weight of potatoes would not prevent each cook or housewife from dressing and serving them in any way she pleased. And we know that stock made from meat can be converted into a hundred different soups to suit a hundred different tastes.

But though we are quite aware of all these facts, we still maintain that no one has a right to force the housewife to take her potatoes from the communal kitchen ready cooked if she prefers to cook them herself in her own pot on her own fire. And, above all, we should wish each one to be free to take his meals with his family, or with his friends, or even in a restaurant, if so it seemed good to him.

Naturally large public kitchens will spring up to take the place of the restaurants, where people are poisoned nowadays. Already the Parisian housewife gets the stock for her soup from the butcher and transforms it into whatever soup she likes, and London housekeepers know that they can have a joint roasted, or an apple or rhubarb tart baked at the baker's for a trifling sum, thus economizing time and fuel. And when the communal kitchen—the common bakehouse of the future—is established, and people can get their food cooked without the risk of being cheated or poisoned, the custom will no doubt become general of going to the communal kitchen for the fundamental parts of the meal, leaving the last touches to be added as individual taste shall suggest.

But to make a hard and fast rule of this, to make a duty of taking home our food ready cooked, that would be as repugnant to our modern minds as the ideas of the convent or the barrack—morbid ideas born in brains warped by tyranny or superstition.

Who will have a right to the food of the commune? will assuredly be the first question which we shall have to ask ourselves. Every township will answer for itself, and we are convinced that the answers will all be dictated by the sentiment of justice. Until labour is reorganized, as long as the disturbed period lasts, and while it is impossible to distinguish between inveterate idlers and genuine workers thrown out of work, the available food ought to be shared by all without exception. Those who have been enemies to the new order will hasten of their own accord to rid the commune of their presence. But it seems to us that the masses of the people, which have always been magnanimous, and have nothing of vindictiveness in their disposition, will be ready to share their bread with all who remain with them, conquered and conquerors alike. It will be no loss to the Revolution to be inspired by such an idea, and, when work is set agoing again, the antagonists of yesterday will stand side by side in the same workshops. A society where work is free will have nothing to fear from idlers.

"But provisions will run short in a month!" our critics at once exclaim.

"So much the better," say we. It will prove that for the first time on record the people have had enough to eat. As to the question of obtaining fresh supplies, we shall discuss the means in our next chapter.

V

By what means could a city in a state of revolution be supplied with food? We shall answer this question, but it is obvious that the means resorted to will depend on the character of the Revolution in the provinces, and in neighbouring countries. If the entire nation, or, better still, if all Europe should accomplish the Social Revolution simultaneously, and start with thorough-going Communism, our procedure would be simplified; but if only a few communities in Europe make the attempt, other means will have to be chosen. The circumstances will dictate the measures.

We are thus led, before we proceed further, to glance at the state of Europe, and, without pretending to prophesy, we may try to foresee what course the Revolution will take, or at least what will be its essential features.

Certainly it would be very desirable that all Europe should rise at once, that expropriation should be general, and that communistic principles should inspire all and sundry. Such a universal rising would do much to simplify the task of our century.

But all the signs lead us to believe that it will not take place. That the Revolution will embrace Europe we do not doubt. If one of the four great continental capitals—Paris, Vienna, Brussels, or Berlin—rises in revolution and overturns its Government, it is almost certain that the three others will follow its example within a few weeks' time. It is, moreover, highly probable that the Peninsulas and even London and St. Petersburg would not be long in following suit. But whether the Revolution would everywhere exhibit the same characteristics is doubtful.

Though it is more than probable that expropriation will be everywhere carried into effect on a larger or smaller scale, and that this policy carried out by any one of the great nations of Europe will influence all the rest; yet the beginnings of the Revolution will exhibit great local differences, and its course will vary in different countries. In 1789-93, the French peasantry took four years to finally rid themselves of the redemption of feudal rights, and the bourgeois to overthrow royalty. Let us keep that in mind, therefore, and be prepared to see the Revolution develop itself somewhat gradually. Let us not be disheartened if here and there its steps should move less rapidly. Whether it would take an avowedly socialist character in all European nations, at any rate at the beginning, is doubtful. Germany, be it remembered, is still realizing its dream of a United Empire. Its advanced parties see visions of a Jacobin Republic like that of 1848, and of the organization of labour according to Louis Blanc; while the French people, on the other hand, want above all things a free Commune, whether it be a communist Commune or not.

There is every reason to believe that, when the coming Revolution takes place, Germany will go further than France went in 1793. The eighteenth century Revolution in France was an advance on the English Revolution of the seventeenth, abolishing as it did at one stroke the power of the throne and the landed aristocracy, whose influence still survives in England. But, if Germany goes further and does greater things than France did in 1793, there can be no doubt that the ideas which will foster the birth of her Revolution will be those of 1848, as the ideas which will inspire the Revolution in Russia will be those of 1789, modified somewhat by the intellectual movements of our own century.

Without, however, attaching to these forecast a greater importance than they merit, we may safely conclude this much: the Revolution will take a different character in each of the different European nations; the point attained in the socialization of wealth will not be everywhere the same.

Will it therefore be necessary, as is sometimes suggested, that the nations in the vanguard of the movement should adapt their pace to those who lag behind? Must we wait till the Communist Revolution is ripe in all civilized countries? Clearly not! Even if it were a thing to be desired it is not possible. History does not wait for the laggards.

Besides, we do not believe that in any one country the Revolution will be accomplished at a stroke, in the twinkling of an eye, as some socialists dream. It is highly probable that if one of the five or six large towns of France—Paris, Lyons, Marseilles, Lille, Saint-Etienne, Bordeaux—were to proclaim the Commune, the others would follow its example, and that many, smaller towns would do the same. Probably also various mining districts and industrial centres would hasten to rid themselves of "owners" and "masters," and form themselves into free groups.

But many country places have not advanced to that point. Side by side with the revolutionized communes such places would remain in an expectant attitude, and would go on living on the Individualist system. Undisturbed by visits of the bailiff or the tax-collector, the peasants would not be hostile to the revolutionaries, and thus, while profiting by the new state of affairs they would defer the settlement of accounts with the local exploiters: But with that practical enthusiasm which always characterizes agrarian uprisings (witness the passionate toil of 1792) they would throw themselves into the task of cultivating the land, which, freed from taxes and mortgages, would become so much dearer to them.

As to abroad, revolution would break out every where, but revolution under divers aspects, in one country State Socialism, in another Federation; everywhere more or less Socialism, not conforming to any particular rule.

VI

Let us now return to our city in revolt, and consider how its citizens can provide foodstuffs for themselves. How are the necessary provisions to be obtained if the nation as a whole has not accepted Communism? This is the question to be solved. Take, for example, one of the large French towns—take the capital itself, for that matter. Paris consumes every year thousands of tons of grain, 350,000 head of oxen, 200,000 calves, 300,000 swine, and more than two millions of sheep, besides great quantities of game. This huge city devours, besides, 18 million pounds of butter, 172 million eggs, and other produce in like proportion.

It imports flour and grain from the United States and from Russia, Hungary, Italy, Egypt, and the Indies; live stock from Germany, Italy, Spain—even Roumania and Russia; and as for groceries, there is not a country in the world that it does not lay under contribution. Now, let us see how Paris or any other great town could be revictualled by home-grown produce, supplies of which could be readily and willingly sent in from the provinces.

To those who put their trust in "authority" the question will appear quite simple. They would begin by establishing a strongly centralized Government, furnished wvith all the machinery of coercion—the police, the army, the guillotine. This Government would draw up a statement of all the produce contained in France. It would divide the country into districts of supply, and then *command* that a prescribed quantity of some particular foodstuff be sent to such a place on such a day, and delivered at such a station, to be there received on a given day by a specified official and stored in particular warehouses.

Now, we declare with the fullest conviction, not merely that such a solution is undesirable, but that it never could by any possibility be put into practice. It is wildly Utopian!

Pen in hand, one may dream such a dream in the study, but in contact with reality it comes to nothing; for, like all such theories, it leaves out of account the spirit of independence that is in man. The attempt would lead to a universal uprising, to three or four *Vendées,* to the villages rising against the towns, all the country up in arms defying the city for its arrogance in attempting to impose such a system upon the country.

We have already had too much of Jacobin Utopias! Let us see if some other form of organization will meet the case.

In 1793 the provinces starved the large towns, and killed the Revolution. And yet it is a known fact that the production of grain in France during 1792-93 had not diminished; indeed the evidence goes to show that it had increased. But after having taken possession of the manorial lands, after having reaped a harvest from them, the peasants would not part with their grain for paper-money. They withheld their produce, waiting for a rise in the price, or the introduction of gold. The most rigorous measures of the National Convention were without avail, and even the fear of death failed to break up the ring, or force its members to sell their corn. For it is matter of history that the commissaries of the Convention did not scruple to guillotine those who withheld their grain from the market, and pitilessly executed those who speculated in foodstuffs. All the same, the corn was not forthcoming, and the townsfolk suffered from famine.

But what was offered to the husbandman in exchange for his hard toil? Assignats, scraps of paper decreasing in value every day, promises of payment, which could not be kept. A forty-pound note would not purchase a pair of boots, and the peasant, very naturally, was not anxious to barter a year's toil for a piece of paper with which he could not even buy a shirt.

As long as worthless paper money—whether called assignats or labour notes—is offered to the peasant-producer it will always be the same. The country will withhold its produce, and the towns will suffer want, even if the recalcitrant peasants are guillotined as before.

We must offer to the peasant in exchange for his toil not worthless paper money, but the manufactured articles of which he stands in immediate need. He lacks the proper implements to till the land, clothes to protect him properly from the inclemencies of the weather, lamps and oil to replace his miserable rushlight or tallow dip, spades, rakes, ploughs. All these things, under present conditions, the peasant is forced to do without, not because he does not feel the need of them, but because, in his life of struggle and privation, a thousand useful things are beyond his reach; because he has no money to buy them.

Let the town apply itself, without loss of time, to manufacturing all that the peasant needs, instead of fashioning gewgaws for the wives of rich citizens. Let the sewing machines of Paris be set to work on clothes for the country-folk: workaday clothes and clothes for Sunday too, instead of costly evening dresses. Let the factories and foundries turn out agricultural implements, spades, rakes, and such-like, instead of waiting till the English send them to France, in exchange for French wines!

Let the towns send no more inspectors to the villages, wearing red, blue, or rainbow-coloured scarves, to convey to the peasant orders to take his produce to this place or that, but let them send friendly embassies to the country-folk and bid them in brotherly fashion: "Bring us your produce, and take from our stores and shops all the manufactured articles you please." Then provisions would pour in on every side. The peasant would only withhold what he needed for his own use, and would send the rest into the cities, feeling *for the first time in the course of history* that these toiling townsfolk were his comrades—his brethren, and not his exploiters.

We shall be told, perhaps, that this would necessitate a complete transformation of industry. Well, yes, that is true of certain departments; but there are other branches which could be rapidly modified in such a way as to furnish the peasant with clothes, watches, furniture, and the simple implements for which the towns make him pay such exorbitant prices at the present time. Weavers, tailors, shoemakers, tinsmiths, cabinet-makers, and many other trades and crafts could easily direct their energies to the manufacture of useful and necessary articles, and abstain from producing mere luxuries. All that is needed is that the public mind should be thoroughly convinced of the necessity of this transformation, and should come to look upon it as an act of justice and of progress, and that it should no longer allow itself to be cheated by that dream, so dear to the theorists—the dream of a revolution which confines itself to taking possession of the profits of industry, and leaves production and commerce just as they are now.

This, then, is our view of the whole question. Cheat the peasant no longer with scraps of paper—be the sums inscribed upon them ever so large; but offer him in exchange for his produce the very things of which he, the tiller of the soil, stands in need. Then the fruits of the land will be poured into the towns. If this is not done there will be famine in our cities, and reaction and despair will follow in its train.

VII

All the great towns, we have said, buy their grain, their flour, and their meat, not only from the provinces, but also from abroad. Foreign countries send Paris spices, fish, and various dainties, besides immense quantities of corn and meat.

But when the Revolution comes we must depend on foreign countries as little as possible. If Russian wheat, Italian or Indian rice, and Spanish or Hungarian wines abound in the markets of western Europe, it is not that the countries which export them have a superabundance, or that such a produce grows there of itself, like the dandelion in the meadows. In Russia, for instance, the peasant works sixteen hours a day, and half starves from three to six months every year, in order to export the grain with which he pays the landlord and the State. To-day the police appears in the Russian village as soon as the harvest is gathered in, and sells the peasant's last horse and last cow for arrears of taxes and rent due to the landlord, unless the victim immolates himself of his own accord by selling the grain to the exporters. Usually, rather than part with his live stock at a disadvantage, he keeps only a nine months' supply of grain, and sells the rest. Then, in order to sustain life until the next harvest, he mixes birch-bark and tares with his flour for three months, if it has been a good year, and for six if it has been bad, while in London they are eating biscuits made of his wheat.

But as soon as the Revolution comes, the Russian peasant will keep bread enough for himself and his children; the Italian and Hungarian peasants will do the same; and the Hindoo, let us hope, will profit by these good examples; and the farmers of America will hardly be able to cover all the deficit in grain which Europe will experience. So it will not do to count on their contributions of wheat and maize satisfying all the wants.

Since all our middle-class civilization is based on the exploitation of inferior races and countries with less advanced industrial systems, the Revolution will confer a boon at the very outset, by menacing that "civilization," and allowing the so-called inferior races to free themselves.

But this great benefit will manifest itself by a steady and marked diminution of the food supplies pouring into the great cities of western Europe.

It is difficult to predict the course of affairs in the provinces. On the one hand the slave of the soil will take advantage of the Revolution to straighten his bowed back. Instead of working fourteen or fifteen hours a day, as he does at present, he will be at liberty to work only half that time, which of course would have the effect of decreasing the production of the principal articles of consumption—grain and meat.

But, on the other hand, there will be an increase of production as soon as the peasant realizes that he is no longer forced to support the idle rich by his toil. New tracts of land will be cleared, new and improved machines set a-going.

"Never was the land so energetically cultivated as in 1792, when the peasant had taken back from the landlord the soil which he had coveted so long," Michelet tells us, speaking of the Great Revolution.

Before long, intensive culture would be within the reach of all. Improved machinery, chemical manures, and all such matters would be common property. But everything tends to indicate that at the outset there would be a falling off in agricultural products, in France as elsewhere.

In any case it would be wisest to count upon such a falling off of contributions from the provinces as well as from abroad.

And how is this falling off to be made good? Why, in heaven's name, by setting to work ourselves! No need to rack our brains for far-fetched panaceas when the remedy lies close at hand!

The large towns must undertake to till the soil, like the country districts. We must return to what biology calls "the integration of functions"—after the division of labour the taking up of it as a whole—this is the course followed throughout Nature.

Besides, philosophy apart, the force of circumstances would bring about this result. Let Paris see that at the end of eight months it will be running short of bread, and Paris will set to work to grow wheat.

"What about land?" It will not be wanting, for it is round the great towns, and round Paris especially, that the parks and pleasure grounds of the landed gentry are to be found. These thousands of acres only await the skilled labour of the husbandman to surround Paris with fields infinitely more fertile and productive than the steppes of southern Russia, where the soil is dried up by the sun. Nor will labour be lacking. To what should the two million citizens of Paris turn their attention when they would be no longer catering for the luxurious fads and amusements of Russian princes, Roumanian grandees, and wives of Berlin financiers?

With all the mechanical inventions of the century; with all the intelligence and technical skill of the worker accustomed to deal with complicated machinery; with inventors, chemists, professors of botany, practical botanists like the market gardeners of Gennevilliers; with all the plant that they could use for multiplying and improving machinery, and, finally, with the organizing spirit of the Parisian people, their pluck and energy—with all these at its command, the agriculture of the anarchist Com mune of Paris would be a very different thing from the rude husbandry of the Ardennes.

Steam, electricity, the heat of the sun, and the breath of the wind, will ere long be pressed into service. The steam harrow and the steam plough will quickly do the rough work of preparation, and the soil, thus cleaned and enriched, will only need the intelligent care of man, and of woman even more than man, to be clothed with luxuriant vegetation—not once but three or four times in the year.

Thus, learning the art of horticulture from experts, and trying experiments in different methods on small patches of soil reserved for the purpose, vying with each other to obtain the best returns, finding in physical exercise, without exhaustion or overwork, the health and strength which so often flags in cities,—men, women, and children will gladly turn to the labour of the fields, when it is no longer a slavish drudgery, but has become pleasure, a festival, a renewal of health and joy.

"There are no barren lands; the earth is worth what man is worth"—that is the last word of modern agriculture. Ask of the earth and she will give you bread, provided that you ask aright.

A district, though it were as small as the depart ments of the Seine and the Seine-et-Oise, and with so great a city as Paris to feed, would be practically sufficient to grow upon it all the food supplies, which otherwise might fail to reach it.

The combination of agriculture and industry, the husbandman and the mechanic in the same individual—this is what anarchist communism will inevitably lead us to, if it starts fair with expropriation.

Let the Revolution only get so far, and famine is not the enemy it will have to fear. No, the danger which will menace it lies in timidity, prejudice, and hali-measures. The danger is where Danton saw it when he cried to France: "Dare, dare, and yet again, dare!" The bold thought first, and the bold deed will not fail to follow.

CHAPTER-VI

DWELLINGS

I

Those who have closely watched the growth of certain ideas among the workers must have noticed that on one momentous question—the housing of the people, namely—a definite conclusion is being imperceptibly arrived at. It is a known fact that in the large towns of France, and in many of the smaller ones also, the workers are coming gradually to the conclusion that dwelling-houses are in no sense the property of those whom the State recognizes as their owners.

This idea has evolved naturally in the minds of the people, and nothing will ever convince them again that the "rights of property" ought to extend to houses.

The house was not built by its owner. It was erected, decorated, and furnished by innumerable workers—in the timber yard, the brick field, and the workshop, toiling for dear life at a minimum wage.

The money spent by the owner was not the product of his own toil. It was amassed, like all other riches, by paying the workers two-thirds or only a half of what was their due.

Moreover and it is here that the enormity of the whole proceeding becomes most glaring—the house owes its actual value to the profit which the owner can make out of it. Now, this profit results from the fact that his house is built in a town possessing bridges, quays, and fine public buildings, and affording to its inhabitants a thousand comforts and conveniences unknown in villages; a town well paved, lighted with gas, in regular communication with other towns, and itself a centre of industry, commerce, science, and art; a town which the work of twenty or thirty generations has gone to render habitable, healthy, and beautiful.

A house in certain parts of Paris may be valued at thousands of pounds sterling, not because thousands of pounds' worth of labour have been expended on that particular house, but because it is in Paris; because for centuries workmen, artists, thinkers, and men of learning and letters have contributed to make Paris what it is to-day—a centre of industry, commerce, politics, art, and science; because Paris has a past; because, thanks to literature, the names of its streets are household words in foreign countries as well as at home; because it is the fruit of eighteen centuries of toil, the work of fifty generations of the whole French nation.

Who, then, can appropriate to himself the tiniest plot of ground, or the meanest building, without committing a flagrant injustice? Who, then, has the right to sell to any bidder the smallest portion of the common heritage?

On that point, as we have said, the workers are agreed. The idea of free dwellings showed its existence very plainly during the siege of Paris, when the cry was for an abatement pure and simple of the terms demanded by the landlords. It appeared again during the Commune of 1871, when the Paris workmen expected the Communal Council to decide boldly on the abolition of rent. And when the New Revolution comes, it will be the first question with which the poor will concern themselves.

Whether in time of revolution or in time of peace, the worker must be housed somehow or other; he must have some sort of roof over his head. But, however tumble-down and squalid your dwelling may be, there is always a landlord who can evict you. True, during the Revolution he cannot find bailiffs and police-serjeants to throw your rags and chattels into the street, but who knows what the new Government will do to-morrow? Who can say that it will not call in the aid of force again, and set the police pack upon you to hound you out of your hovels? We have seen the Commune proclaim the remission of rents due up to the first of April only!* After that rent had to be paid, though Paris was in a state of chaos, and industry at a standstill; so that the revolutionist had absolutely nothing to depend upon but his allowance of fifteen pence a day!

Now the worker must be made to see clearly that in refusing to pay rent to a landlord or owner he is not simply profiting by the disorganization of authority. He must understand that the abolition of rent is a recognized principle, sanctioned, so to speak, by popular assent; that to be housed rent-free is a right proclaimed aloud by the people

Are we going to wait till this measure, which is in harmony with every honest man's sense of justice, is taken up by the few socialists scattered among

* The decree of the 30 March : by this decree rents due up to the terms of October, 1870, and January and April, 1871, were annulled.

the middle-class elements, of which the Provisionary Government will be composed? We should have to wait long—till the return of reaction, in fact!

This is why, refusing uniforms and badges—those outward signs of authority and servitude—and remaining people among the people, the earnest revolutionists will work side by side with the masses, that the abolition of rent, the expropriation of houses, may become an accomplished fact. They will prepare the ground and encourage ideas to grow in this direction; and when the fruit of their labours is ripe, the people will proceed to expropriate the houses without giving heed to the theories which will certainly be thrust in their way—theories about paying compensation to landlords, and finding first the necessary funds.

On the day that the expropriation of houses takes place, on that day, the exploited workers will have realized that the new times have come, that Labour will no longer have to bear the yoke of the rich and powerful, that Equality has been openly proclaimed, that this Revolution is a real fact, and not a theatrical make-believe, like so many others preceding it.

II

If the idea of expropriation be adopted by the people it will be carried into effect in spite of all the "insurmountable" obstacles with which we are menaced.

Of course, the good folk in new uniforms, seated in the offcial arm-chairs of the HÃ´tel de Ville, will be sure to busy themselves in heaping up obstacles. They will talk of giving compensation to the landlords, of preparing statistics, and drawing up long reports. Yes, they would be capable of drawing up reports long enough to outlast the hopes of the people, who, after waiting and starving in enforced idleness, and seeing nothing come of all these official researches, would lose heart and faith in the Revolution and abandon the field to the reactionaries. The new bureaucracy would end by making expropriation hateful in the eyes of all.

Here, indeed, is a rock which might shipwreck our hopes. But if the people turn a deaf ear to the specious arguments used to dazzle them, and realize that new life needs new conditions, and if they undertake the task themselves, then expropriation can be effected without any great difficulty.

"But how? How can it be done?" you ask us. We shall try to reply to this question, but with a reservation. We have no intention of tracing out the plans of expropriation in their smallest details. We know beforehand that all that any man, or group of men, could suggest to-day would be far surpassed by the reality when it comes. Man will accomplish greater things, and accomplish them better and by simpler methods than those dictated to him beforehand.

Thus we are content to indicate the manner by which expropriation might be accomplished without the intervention of Government. We do not propose to go out of our way to answer those who declare that the thing is impossible. We confine ourselves to replying that we are not the upholders of any particular method of organization. We are only concerned to demonstrate that expropriation *could* be effected by popular initiative, and *could not* be effected by any other means whatever.

It seems very likely that, as soon as expropriation is fairly started, groups of volunteers will spring up in every district, street, and block of houses, and undertake to inquire into the number of flats and houses which are empty and of those which are overcrowded, the unwholesome slums and the houses which are too spacious for their occupants and might well be used to house those who are stifled in swarming tenements In a few days these volunteers would have drawn up complete lists for the street and the district of all the flats, tenements, family mansions and villa residences, all the rooms and suites of rooms, healthy and unhealthy, small and large, foetid dens and homes of luxury.

Freely communicating with each other, these volunteers would soon have their statistics complete. False statistics can be manufactured in board rooms and offices, but true and exact statistics must begin with the individual and mount up from the simple to the complex.

Then, without waiting for any one's leave, those citizens will probably go and find their comrades who were living in miserable garrets and hovels and will say to them simply: "It is a real Revolution this time, comrades, and no mistake about it. Come to such a place this evening; all the neighbourhood will be there; we are going to redistribute the dwelling-houses. If you are tired of your slum-garret, come and choose one of the flats of five rooms that are to be disposed of, and when you have once moved in you shall stay, never fear. The people are up in arms, and he who would venture to evict you will have to answer to them."

"But every one will want a fine house or a spacious flat!" we are told. No, you are mistaken. It is not the people's way to clamour for the moon. On the contrary, every time we have seen them set about repairing a wrong we have been struck by the good sense and instinct for justice which animates the masses. Have we ever known them demand the impossible? Have we ever seen the people of Paris fighting among themselves while waiting for their rations of bread or firewood during the two sieges? The patience and resignation which prevailed among them was constantly held up to admiration by the foreign press correspondents; and yet these patient waiters knew full well that the last comers would have to pass the day without food or fire.

We do not deny that there are plenty of egotistic instincts in isolated individuals in our societies. We are quite aware of it. But we contend that the very way to revive and nourish these instincts would be to confine such questions as the housing of the people to any board or committee, in fact, to the tender mercies of officialism in any shape or form. Then indeed all the evil passions spring up, and it becomes a case of who is the most influential person on the board. The least inequality causes wranglings and recriminations. If the smallest advantage is given to any one, a tremendous hue and cry is raised—and not without reason.

But if the people themsevles, organized by streets, districts, and parishes, undertake to move the inhabitants of the slums into the half-empty dwellings of the middle classes, the trifling inconveniences, the little inequalities will be easily tided over. Rarely has appeal been made to the good instincts of the masses—only as a last resort, to save the sinking ship in times of revolution—but never has such an appeal been made in vain; the heroism, the self-devotion of the toiler has never failed to respond to it. And thus it will be in the coming Revolution.

But, when all is said and done, some inequalities, some inevitable injustices, will remain. There are individuals in our societies whom no great crisis can lift out of the deep ruts of egoism in which they are sunk. The question, however, is not whether there will be injustices or no, but rather how to limit the number of them.

Now all history, all the experience of the human race, and all social psychology, unite in showing that the best and fairest way is to trust the decision to those whom it concerns most nearly. It is they alone who can consider and allow for the hundred and one details which must necessarily be overlooked in any merely official redistribution.

III

Moreover, it is by no means necessary to make straightway an absolutely equal redistribution of all the dwellings. There will no doubt be some inconveniences at first, but matters will soon be righted in a society which has adopted expropriation.

When the masons, and carpenters, and all who are concerned in house building, know that their daily bread is secured to them, they will ask nothing better than to work at their old trades a few hours a day. They will adapt the fine houses which absorbed the time of a whole staff of servants, and in a few months homes will have sprung up, infinitely healthier and more conveniently arranged than those of to-day. And to those who are not yet comfortably housed the anarchist Commune will be able to say: "Patience, comrades! Palaces fairer and finer than any the capitalists built for themselves will spring from the ground of our enfranchised city. They will belong to those who have most need of them. The anarchist Commune does not build with an eye to revenues.

These monuments erected to its citizens, products of the collective spirit, will serve as models to all humanity; they will be yours."

If the people of the Revolution expropriate the houses and proclaim free lodgings—the communalizing of houses and the right of each family to a decent dwelling—then the Revolution will have assumed a communistic character from the first, and started on a course from which it will be by no means easy to turn it. It will have struck a fatal blow at individual property.

For the expropriation of dwellings contains in germ the whole social revolution. On the manner of its accomplishment depends the character of all that follows. Either we shall start on a good road leading straight to anarchist communism, or we shall remain sticking in the mud of despotic individualism.

It is easy to see the numerous objections—theoretic on the one hand, practical on the other—with which we are sure to be met. As it will be a question of maintaining iniquity at any price, our opponents will of course protest "in the name of justice." "Is it not a crying shame," they will exclaim, "that the people of Paris should take possession of all these fine houses, while the peasants in the country have only tumble-down huts to live in?" But do not let us make a mistake. These enthusiasts for justice forget, by a lapse of memory to which they are subject, the "crying shame" which they themselves are tacitly defending. They forget that in this same city the worker, with his wife and children, suffocates in a noisome garret, while from his window he sees the rich man's palace. They forget that whole generations perish in crowded slums, starving for air and sunlight, and that to redress this injustice ought to be the first task of the Revolution.

Do not let these disingenuous protests hold us back. We know that any inequality which may exist between town and country in the early days of the Revolution will be transitory and of a nature to right itself from day to day; for the village will not fail to improve its dwellings as soon as the peasant has ceased to be the beast of burden of the farmer, the merchant, the money-lender, and the State. In order to avoid an accidental and transitory inequality, shall we stay our hand from righting an ancient wrong?

The so-called practical objections are not very formidable either. We are bidden to consider the hard case of some poor fellow who by dint of privation has contrived to buy a house just large enough to hold his family. And we are going to deprive him of his hard-earned happiness, to turn him into the street! Certainly not. If his house is only just large enough for his family, by all means let him stay there. Let him work in his little garden too; our "boys" will not hinder him—nay, they will lend him a helping hand if need be. But suppose he lets lodgings, suppose he has empty rooms in his house; then the people will make the lodger understand that he need not pay his former landlord any more rent. Stay where you are, but rent free. No more duns and collectors; Socialism has abolished all that!

Or again, suppose that the landlord has a score of rooms all to himself, and some poor woman lives near by with five children in one room. In that case the people would see whether, with some alterations, these empty rooms could not be converted into a suitable home for the poor woman and her five children. Would not that be more just and fair than to leave the mother and her five little ones languishing in a garret, while Sir Gorgeous Midas sat at his ease in an empty mansion? Besides, good Sir Gorgeous would probably hasten to do it of his own accord; his wife will be delighted to be freed from half her big, unwieldy house when there is no longer a staff of servants to keep it in order.

"So you are going to turn everything upside down." say the defenders of law and order. "There will be no end to the evictions and removals. Would it not be better to start fresh by turning everybody out of doors and redistributing the houses by lot?" Thus our critics; but we are firmly persuaded that if no Government interferes in the matter, if all the changes are entrusted to those free groups which have sprung up to undertake the work, the evictions and removals will be less numerous than those which take place in one year under the present system, owing to the rapacity of landlords.

In the first place, there are in all large towns almost enough empty houses and flats to lodge all the inhabitants of the slums. As to the palaces and suites of fine apartments, many working people would not live in them if they could. One could not "keep up" such houses without a large staff of servants. Their occupants would soon find themselves forced to seek less luxurious dwellings. The fine ladies would find that palaces were not well adapted to self-help in the kitchen. Gradually people would shake down. There would be no need to conduct Dives to a garret at the bayonet's point, or install Lazarus in Dives's palace by the help of an armed escort. People would shake down amicably into the available dwellings with the least possible friction and disturbance. Have we not the example of the village communes redistributing fields and disturbing the owners of the allotments so little that one can only praise the intelligence and good sense of the methods they employ. Fewer fields change hands under the management of the Russian Commune than where personal property holds sway, and is for ever carrying its quarrels into courts of law. And are we to believe that the inhabitants of a great European city would be less intelligent and less capable of organization than Russian or Hindoo peasants?

Moreover, we must not blink the fact that every revolution means a certain disturbance to everyday life, and those who expect this tremendous lift out of the old grooves to be accomplished without so much as jarring the dishes on their dinner tables will find themselves mistaken. It is true that Governments can change without disturbing worthy citizens at dinner, but the crimes of society towards those who have nourished and supported it are not to be redressed by any such political sleight of parties.

Undoubtedly there will be a disturbance, but it must not be of pure destruction; it must be minimized. And again—it is impossible to lay too much stress on this maxim—it will be by addressing ourselves to the interested parties, and not to boards and committees, that we shall best succeed in reducing the sum of inconveniences for everybody.

The people commit blunder on blunder when they have to choose by ballot some hare-brained candidate who solicits the honour of representing them, and takes upon himself to know all, to do all, and to organize all. But when they take upon themselves to organize what they know, what touches them directly, they do it better than all the "talking-shops" put together. Is not the Paris Commune an instance in point? and the great dockers' strike? and have we not constant evidence of this fact in every village commune?

CHAPTER-VII

CLOTHING

I

When the houses have become the common heritage of the citizens, and when each man has his daily supply of food, another forward step will have to be taken. The question of clothing will of course demand consideration next, and again the only possible solution will be to take possession, in the name of the people, of all the shops and warehouses where clothing is sold or stored, and to throw open the doors to all, so that each can take what he needs. The communalization of clothing—the right of each to take what he needs from the communal stores, or to have it made for him at the tailors and outfitters—is a necessary corollary of the communalization of houses and food.

Obviously we shall not need for that to despoil all citizens of their coats, to put all the garments in a heap and draw lots for them, as our critics, with equal wit and ingenuity, suggest. Let him who has a coat keep it still—nay, if he have ten coats it is highly improbable that any one will want to deprive him of them, for most folk would prefer a new coat to one that has already graced the shoulders of some fat bourgeois; and there will be enough new garments and to spare, without having recourse to second-hand wardrobes.

If we were to take an inventory of all the clothes and stuff for clothing accumulated in the shops and stores of the large towns, we should find probably that in Paris, Lyons, Bordeaux, and Marseilles, there was enough to enable the commune to offer garments to all the citizens, of both sexes; and if all were not suited at once, the communal outfitters would soon make good these shortcomings. We know how rapidly our great tailoring and dressmaking establishments work nowadays, provided as they are with machinery specially adapted for production on a large scale.

"But every one will want a sable-lined coat or a velvet gown!" exclaim our adversaries.

Frankly, we do not believe it. Every woman does not dote on velvet, nor does every man dream of sable linings. Even now, if we were to ask each woman to choose her gown, we should find some to prefer a simple, practical garment to all the fantastic trimmings the fashionable world affects.

Tastes change with the times, and the fashion in vogue at the time of the Revolution will certainly make for simplicity. Societies, like individuals, have their hours of cowardice, but also their heroic moments; and though the society of to-day cuts a very poor figure sunk in the pursuit of narrow personal interests and second-rate ideas, it wears a different air when great crises come. It has its moments of greatness and enthusiasm. Men of generous nature will gain the power which to-day is in the hand of jobbers. Self-devotion will spring up, and noble deeds beget their like; even the egotists will be ashamed of hanging back, and will be drawn in spite of themselves to admire, if not to imitate, the generous and brave.

The great Revolution of 1793 abounds in examples of this kind, and it is ever during such times of spiritual revival—as natural to societies as to individuals—that the spring-tide of enthusiasm sweeps humanity onwards.

We do not wish to exaggerate the part played by such noble passions, nor is it upon them that we would found our ideal of society. But we are not asking too much if we expect their aid in tiding over the first and most difficult moments. We cannot hope that our daily life will be continuously inspired by such exalted enthusiasms, but we may expect their aid at the first, and that is all we need.

It is just to wash the earth clean, to sweep away the shards and refuse, accumulated by centuries of slavery and oppression, that the new anarchist society will have need of this wave of brotherly love. Later on it can exist without appealing to the spirit of self-sacrifice, because it will have eliminated oppression, and thus created a new world instinct with all the feelings of solidarity.

Besides, should the character of the Revolution be such as we have sketched here, the free initiative of individuals would find an extensive field of action in thwarting the efforts of the egotists. Groups would spring up in every street and quarter to undertake the charge of the clothing. They would make inventories of all that the city possessed, and would find out approximately what were the resources at their disposal. It is more than likely that in the matter of clothing the citizens would adopt the same principle as in the matter of provisions—that is to say, they would offer freely from the common store everything which was to be found in abundance, and dole out whatever was limited in quantity.

Not being able to offer to each man a sable-lined coat, and to every woman a velvet gown, society would probably distinguish between the superfluous and the necessary, and, provisionally, at least, class sable and velvet among the superfluities of life, ready to let time prove whether what is a luxury to-day may not become common to all to-morrow. While the necessary clothing would be guaranteed to each inhabitant of the anarchist city, it would be left to private activity to provide for the sick and feeble those things, provisionally considered as luxuries, and to procure for the less robust such special articles, as would not enter into the daily consumption of ordinary citizens.

"But," it may be urged, "this grey uniformity means the end of everything beautiful in life and art. "

"Certainly not!" we reply; and we still base our opinion on what already exists. We propose to show presently how an Anarchist society could satisfy the most artistic tastes of its citizens without allowing them to amass the fortunes of millionaires.

CHAPTER-VIII

WAYS AND MEANS

I

If a society, a city, or a territory, were to guaran tee the necessaries of life to its inhabitants (and we shall see how the conception of the necessaries of life can be so extended as to include luxuries), it would be compelled to take possession of what is absolutely needed for production; that is to say— land, machinery, factories, means of transport, etc. Capital in the hands of private owners would be expropriated and returned to the community.

The great harm done by bourgeois society, as we have already mentioned, is not only that capitalists seize a large share of the profits of each industrial and commercial enterprise, thus enabling them to live without working, but that all production has taken a wrong direction, as it is not carried on with a view to securing well-being to all. For this reason we condemn it.

Moreover, it is impossible to carry on mercantile production in everybody's interest. To wish it would be to expect the capitalist to go beyond his province and to furfil duties that he cannot fulfil without ceasing to be what he is—a private manufacturer seeking his own enrichment. Capitalist organization, based on the personal interest of each individual trader, has given all that could be expected of it to society—it has increased the productive force of work. The capitalist, profiting by the revolution effected in industry by steam, by the sudden development of chemistry and machinery, and by other inventions of our century, has endeavoured in his own interest to increase the yield of work, and in a great measure he has succeeded. But to attribute other duties to him would be unreasonable. For example, to expect that he should use this superior yield of work in the interest of society as a whole, would be to ask philanthropy and charity of him, and a capitalist enterprise *cannot* be based on charity.

It now remains for society to extend this greater productivity, which is limited to certain industries, and to apply it to the general good. But it is evident that to guarantee well-being to all, society must take back possession of all means of production.

Economists, as is their wont, will not fail to remind us of the comparative well-being of a certain category of young robust workmen, skilled in certain special branches of industry. It is always this minority that is pointed out to us with pride. But is this well-being, which is the exclusive right of a few, secure? To-morrow, maybe, negligence, improvidence, or the greed of their employers, will deprive these privileged men of their work, and they will pay for the period of comfort they have enjoyed with months and years of poverty or destitution. How many important industries—woven goods, iron, sugar, etc.—without mentioning short-lived trades, have we not seen decline or come to a standstill alternately on account of speculations, or in consequence of natural displacement of work, and lastly from the effects of competition due to capitalists them selves! If the chief weaving and mechanical industries had to pass through such a crisis as they have passed through in 1886, we hardly need mention the small trades, all of which come periodically to a standstill.

What, too, shall we say to the price which is paid for the relative well-being of certain categories of workmen? Unfortunately, it is paid for by the ruin of agriculture, the shameless exploitation of the peasants, the misery of the masses. In comparison with the feeble minority of workers who enjoy a certain comfort, how many millions of human beings live from hand to mouth, without a secure wage, ready to go wherever they are wanted; how many peasants work fourteen hours a day for a poor pittance! Capital depopulates the country, exploits the colonies and the countries where industries are but little developed, dooms the immense majority of workmen to remain without technical education, to remain mediocre even in their own trade.

This is not merely accidental, it is a *necessity* of the capitalist system. In order to remunerate certain classes of workmen, peasants *must* be come the beasts of burden of society; the country *must* be deserted for the town; small trades must agglomerate in the foul suburbs of large cities, and manufacture a thousand things of little value for next to nothing, so as to bring the goods of the greater industries within reach of buyers with small salaries. That bad cloth may sell, garments are made for ill-paid workers by tailors who are satisfied with a starvation wage! Eastern lands in a backward state are exploited by the West, in order that, under the capitalist system, workers in a few privileged industries may obtain certain limited comforts of life.

The evil of the present system is therefore not that the "surplus-value" of production goes to the capitalist, as Rodbertus and Marx said, thus narrowing the Socialist conception and the general view of the capitalist system; the surplus-value itself is but a consequence of deeper causes. The evil lies *in the possibility of a surplus-value existing,* instead of a simple surplus not consumed by each generation; for, that a surplus-value should exist, means that men, women, and children are compelled by hunger to sell their labour for a small part of what this labour produces, and, above all, of what their labour is capable of producing. But this evil will last as long as the instruments of production belong to a few. As long as men are compelled to pay tribute to property holders for the right of cultivating land or putting machinery into action, and the property holder is free to produce what bids fair to bring him in the greatest profits, rather than the greatest amount of useful commodities—well-being can only be temporarily guaranteed to a very few, and is only to be bought by the poverty of a section of society. It is not sufficient to distribute the profits realized by a trade in equal parts, if at the same time thousands of other workers are exploited. It is a case of PRODUCING THE GREATEST AMOUNT OF GOODS NECESSARY TO THE WELL-BEING OF ALL, WITH THE LEAST POSSIBLE WASTE OF HUMAN ENERGY.

This cannot be the aim of a private owner; and this is why society as a whole, taking this view of production as its ideal, will be compelled to expropriate all that enhances well-being while producing wealth. It will have to take possession of land, factories, mines, means of communication, etc., and besides, it will have to study what products will promote general well-being, as well as the ways and means of production.

II

How many hours a day will man have to work to produce nourishing food, a comfortable home, and necessary clothing for his family? This question has often preoccupied Socialists, and they generally came to the conclusion that four or five hours a day would suffice, on condition, be it well undertsood, that all men work. At the end of last century, Benjamin Franklin fixed the limit at five hours; and if the need of comfort is greater now, the power of production has augmented too, and far more rapidly.

In speaking of agriculture further on, we shall see what the earth can be made to yield to man when he cultivates it scientifically, instead of throwing seed haphazard in a badly ploughed soil as he mostly does to-day. In the great farms of Western America, some of which cover 30 square miles, but have a poorer soil than the manured soil of civilized countries, only 10 to 15 English bushels per English acre are obtained; that is to say, half the yield of European farms or of American farms in Eastern States. And never theless, thanks to machines which enable 2 men to plough 4 English acres a day, 100 men can produce in a year all that is necessary to deliver the bread of 10,000 people at their homes during a whole year.

Thus it would suffice for a man to work under tte same conditions for 30 *hours*, say 6 *half-days of five hours each, to have bread for a whole year;* and to work 30 half-days to guarantee the same to a famity of 5 people.

We shall also prove by results obtained now adays that if we had recourse to intensive agriculture, less than 6 half-days' work could procure bread, meat, vegetables, and even luxurious fruit for a whole family.

And again, if we study the cost of workmen's dwellings, built in large towns to-day, we can ascertain that to obtain, in a large English city, a detached little house, as they are built for workmen, from 1400 to 1800 half-days' work of 5 hours would be sufficient. As a house of that kind lasts 50 years at least, it follows that 28 to 36 half-days' work a year would provide well-furnished, healthy quarters, with all necessary comfort for a family. Whereas when hiring the same apartment from an employer, a workman pays 75 to 1OO days' work per year.

Mark that these figures represent the maximum of what a house costs in England to-day, being given the defective organization of our societies. In Belgium, workmen's cities have been built far cheaper. Taking everything into consideration, we are justified in affirming that in a well-organized society 30 or 40 half-days' work a year will suffice to guarantee a perfectly comfortable home.

There now remains clothing, the exact value of which is almost impossible to fix, because the profits realized by a swarm of middlemen cannot be estimated. Let us take cloth, for example, and add up all the deductions made by landowners, sheep owners, wool merchants, and all their intermediate agents, then by railway companies, mill-owners, weavers, dealers in ready-made clothes, sellers and commission agents, and you will get an idea of what is paid to a whole swarm of capitalists for each article of clothing. That is why it is perfectly impossible to say how many days' work an overcoat that you pay £3 or £4 in a. large London shop represents.

What is certain is that with present machinery they no doubt manage to manufacture an incredible amount of goods.

A few examoles will suffice. Thus in the United States, in 751 cotton mills (for spinning and weav ing), 175,000 men and women produce 2,033,000,000 yards of cotton goods, besides a great quantity of thread. On the average, more than 12,000 yards of cotton goods alone are obtained by a 300 days' work of 9½ hours each, say 40 yards of cotton in 10 hours. Admitting that a family needs 200 yards a year at most, this would be equivalent to 50 hours' work, say 10 *half-days of 5 hours each.* And we should have thread besides; that is to say, cotton to sew with, and thread to weave cloth with, so as to manufacture woolen stuffs mixed with cotton.

As to the results obtained by weaving alone, the official statistics of the United States teach us that in 1870 if workmen worked 13 to 14 hours a day, they made 1O,OOO yards of white cotton goods in a year; thirteen years later (1886) they wove 30,000 yards by working only 55 hours a week.

Even in printed cotton goods they obtained, weaving and printing included, 32,000 yards in 2670 hours of work a year—say about 12 yards an hour. Thus to have your 200 yards of white and printed cotton goods 17 *hours'* work a year would suffice. It is necessary to remark that raw material reaches these factories in about the same state as it comes from the fields, and that the transformations gone through by the piece before it is converted into goods are completed in the course of these 17 hours. But to *buy* these 200 yards from the tradesman, a well-paid workman must *give at the very* least 1O to 15 days' work of 1O hours each, say 1OO to 150 hours. find as to the English peasant, he would have to toil for a month, or a little more, to obtain this luxury.

By this example we already see that by working *50 half-days per year* in a well-organized society we could dress better than the lower middle classes do to-day.

But with all this we have only required 60 half-days' work of 5 hours each to obtain the fruits of the earth, 40 for housing, and 50 for clothing, which only makes half a year's work, as the year consists of 300 working-days if we deduct holidays.

There remain still 150 half-days' work which could be made use of for other necessaries of life— wine, sugar, coffee, tea, furniture, transport, etc. etc.

It is evident that these calculations are only approximative, but they can also be proved in an other way. When we take into account how many, in the so-called civilized nations, produce nothing, how many work at harmful trades, doomed to disappear, and lastly, how many are only useless middlemen, we see that in each nation the number of real producers could be doubled. And if, instead of every 1O men, 20 were occupied in producing useful commodities, and if society took the trouble to economize human energy, those 20 people would only have to work 5 hours a day without production decreasing. And it would suffice to reduce the waste of human energy at the service of wealthy families, or of those administrations that have one official to every ten inhabitants, and to utilize those forces, to augment the productivity of the nation, to limit work to four or even to three hours, on condition that we should be satisfied with present production.

After studying all these facts together, we may arrive, then, at the following conclusion: Imagine a society, comprising a few million inhabitants, engaged in agriculture and a great variety of industries—Paris, for example, with the Department of Seine-et-Oise. Suppose that in this society all children learn to work with their hands as well as with their brains. Admit that all adults, save women, engaged in the education of their children, bind themselves to work 5 *hours a day* from the age of twenty or twenty-two to forty-five or fifty, and that they follow occupations they have chosen in any one branch of human work considered *necessary.* Such a society could in return guarantee well-being to all its members; that is to say, a more substantial well-being than that enjoyed to-day by the middle classes. And, moreover, each worker belonging to this society would have at his disposal at least 5 hours a day which he could devote to science, art, and individual needs which do not come under the category of *necessities,* but will probably do so later on, when man's productivity will have augmented, and those objects will no longer appear luxurious or inaccessible.

CHAPTER-IX

THE NEED FOR LUXURY

I

MAN, however, is not a being whose exclusive purpose in life is eating, drinking, and providing a shelter for himself. As soon as his material wants are satisfied, other needs, of an artistic character, will thrust themselves forward the more ardently. Aims of life vary with each and every individual; and the more society is civilized, the more will individuality be developed, and the more will desires be varied.

Even to-day we see men and women denying themselves necessaries to acquire mere trifles, to obtain some particular gratification, or some intellectual or material enjoyment. A Christian or an ascetic may disapprove of these desires for luxury; but it is precisely these trifles that break the monotony of existence and make it agreeable. Would life, with all its inevitable sorrows, be worth living, if besides daily work man could never obtain a single pleasure according to his individual tastes?

If we wish for a Social Revolution, it is no doubt in the first place to give bread to all; to transform this execrable society, in which we can every day see robust workmen dangling their arms for want of an employer who will exploit them; women and children wandering shelterless at night; whole families reduced to dry bread; men, women, and children dying for want of care and even for want of food. It is to put an end to these iniquities that we rebel.

But we expect more from the Revolution. We see that the worker compelled to struggle painfully for bare existence, is reduced to ignorance of these higher delights, the highest within man's reach, of science, and especially of scientific discovery; of art, and especially of artistic creation. It is in order to obtain these joys for all, which are now reserved to a few; in order to give leisure and the possibility of developing intellectual capacities, that the social revolution must guarantee daily bread to all. After bread has been secured, leisure is the supreme aim.

No doubt, nowadays, when hundreds and thousands of human beings are in need of bread, coal, clothing, and shelter, luxury is a crime; to satisfy it the worker's child must go without bread! But in a society in which all can eat sufficiently the needs which we consider luxuries to- day will be the more keenly felt. And as all men do not and cannot resemble one another (the variety of tastes and needs is the chief guarantee of human progress) there will always be, and it is desirable that there should always be, men and women whose desire will go beyond those of ordinary individuals in some particular direction.

Everybody does not need a telescope, because, even if learning were general, there are people who prefer examining things through a microscope to studying the starry heavens. Some like statues, some pictures. A particular individual has no other ambition than to possess an excellent piano, while another is pleased with an accordion. The tastes vary, but the artistic needs exist in all. In our present, poor capitalistic society, the man who has artistic needs cannot satisfy them unless he is heir to a large fortune, or by dint of hard work appropriates to himself an intellectual capital which will enable him to take up a liberal profession. Still he cherishes the hopeof some day satisfying his tastes more of less, and for this reason he reproaches the idealist Communist societies with having the material life of each individual as their sole aim.—"In your communal stores you may perhaps have bread for all," he says to us, "but you will not have beautiful pictures, optical instruments, luxurious furniture, artistic jewelry—in short, the many things that minister to the infinite variety of human tastes. And in this way you suppress the possibility of obtaining anything besides the bread and meat which the commune can offer to all, and the grey linen in which all your lady citizens will be dressed."

These are the objections which all communist systems have to consider, and which the founders of new societies, established in American deserts, never understood. They believed that if the community could procure sufficient cloth to dress all its members, a music hall in which the "brothers" could strum a piece of music, or act a play from time to time, it was enough. They forgot that the feeling for art existed in the agriculturist as well as in the burgher, and, notwithstanding that the expression of artistic feeling varies according to the difference in culture, in the main it remains the same. In vain did the community guarantee the common necessaries of life, in vain did it suppress all education that would tend to develop individuality, in vain did it eliminate all reading save the Bible. Individual tastes broke forth, and caused general discontent; quarrels arose when somebody proposed to buy a piano or scientific instruments; and the elements of progress flagged. The society could only exist on condition that it crushed all individual feeling, all artistic tendency, and all development.

Will the anarchist Commune be impelled by the same direction? Evidently not, if it understands that while it produces all that is necessary to material life, it must also strive to satisfy all manifestations of the human mind.

II

We frankly confess that when we think of the abyss of poverty and suffering that surrounds us, when we hear the heartrending cry of the worker walking the streets begging for work, we are loth to discuss the question: How will men act in a society, whose members are properly fed, to satisfy certain individuals desirous of possessing a piece of SÃ¨vres china or a velvet dress?

We are tempted to answer: Let us make sure of bread to begin with, we shall see to china and velvet later on.

But as we must recognize that man has other needs besides food, and as the strength of Anarchy lies precisely in that it understands all human faculties and *all* passions, and ignores none, we shall, in a few words, explain how man can contrive to satisfy all his intellectual and artistic needs.

We have already mentioned that by working 4 or 5 hours a day till the age of forty-five or fifty, man could easily produce *all* that is necessary to guarantee comfort to society.

But the day's work of a man accustomed to toil does not consist of; hours; it is a 10 hours' day for 300 days a year, and lasts all his life. Of course, when a man is harnessed to a machine, his health is soon undermined and his intelligence is blunted; but when man has the possibility of varying occupations, and especially of alternating manual with intellectual work, he can remain occupied without fatigue, and even with pleasure, for 10 or 12 hours a day. Consequently the man who will have done 4 or 5 hours of manual work necessary for his existence, will have before him 5 or 6 hours which he will seek to employ according to his tastes. And these 5 or 6 hours a day will fully enable him to procure for himself, if he associates with others, all he wishes for, in addition to the necessaries guaranteed to all.

He will discharge first his task in the field, the factory, and so on, which he owes to society as his contribution to the general production. And he will employ the second half of his day, his week, or his year, to satisfy his artistic or scientific needs, or his hobbies.

Thousands of societies will spring up to gratify every taste and every possible fancy.

Some, for example, will give their hours of leisure to literature. They will then form groups comprising authors, compositors, printers, engravers, draughtsmen, all pursuing a common aim—the propagation of ideas that are dear to them.

Nowadays an author knows that there is a beast of burden, the worker, to whom, for the sum of a few shillings a day, he can entrust the printing of his books; but he hardly cares to know what a printing office is like. If the compositor suffers from lead-poisoning, and if the child who sees to the machine dies of anÃ¦mia, are there not other poor wretches to replace them?

But when there will be no more starvelings ready to sell their work for a pittance, when the exploited worker of to-day will be educated and will have his *own* ideas to put down in black and white and to communicate to others, then the authors and scientific men will be compelled to combine among themselves and with the printers, in order to bring out their prose and their poetry.

So long as men consider fustian and manual labour as a mark of inferiority, it will appear amazing to them to see an author setting up his own book in type, for has he not a gymnasium or games by way of diversion? But when the opprobrium connected with manual labour has disappeared, when all will have to work with their hands, there being no one to do it for them, then the authors as well as their admirers will soon learn the art of handling composing-sticks and type; they will know the pleasure of coming together—all admirers of the work to be printed—to set up the type, to shape it into pages, to take it in its virginal purity from the press. These beautiful machines, instruments of torture to the child who attends on them from morn till night, will be a source of enjoyment for those who will make use of them in order to give voice to the thoughts of their favourite author.

Will literature lose by it? Will the poet be less a poet after having worked out of doors or helped with his hands to multiply his work? Will the novelist lose his knowledge of human nature after having rubbed shoulders with other men in the forest or the factory, in the laying out of a road or on a railway line? Can there be two answers to these questions?

Maybe some books will be less voluminous; but then, more will be said on fewer pages. Maybe fewer waste-sheets will be published; but the matter printed will be more attentively read and more appreciated. The book will appeal to a larger circle of better educated readers, who will be more competent to judge.

Moreover, the art of printing, that has so little progressed since Gutenberg, is still in its infancy. It takes two hours to compose in type what is written in ten minutes, but more expeditious methods of multiplying thought are being sought after and will be discovered.

What a pity every author does not have to take his share in the printing of his works! What progress printing would have already made! We should no longer be using the movable letters, as in the seventeenth century.

III

Is it a dream to concieve a society in which—all having become producers, all having received an education that enables them to cultivate science or art, and all having leisure to do so—men would combine to publish the works of their choice, by contributing each his share of manual work? We have already hundreds of learned, literary, and other societies; and these societies are nothing but voluntary groups of men, interested in certain branches of learning, and associated for the purpose of publishing their works. The authors who write for the periodicals of these societies are not paid, and the periodicals are not for sale; they are sent gratis to all quarters of the globe, to other societies, cultivating the same branches of learning. This member of the society may insert in its review a one-page note summarizing his observations; another may publish therein an extensive work, the results of long years of study; while others will confine themselves to consulting the review as a startingpoint for further research.It does not matter: all these authors and readers are associated for the production of works in which all of them take an interest.

It is true that a learned society, like the individual author, goes to a printing office where workmen are engaged to do the printing. Nowadays, those who belong to the learned societies despise manual labour; which indeed is carried on under very bad conditions; but a community which would give a generous philosophic and *scientific* education to all its members, would know how to organize manual labour in such a way that it would be the pride of humanity. Its learned societies would become associations of explorers, lovers of science, and workers—all knowing a manual trade and all interested in science.

If, for example, the society is studying geology, all will contribute to the exploration of the earth's strata; each member will take his share in research, and ten thousand observers where we have now only a hundred, will do more in a year than we can do in twenty years. And when their works are to be published, ten thousand men and women, skilled in different trades, will be ready to draw maps, engrave designs, compose, and print the books. With gladness will they give their leisure—in summer to exploration in winter to indoor work And when their works appear, they will find not only a hundred, but ten thousand readers interested in their common work.

This is the direction in which progress is already moving. Even to-day, when England felt the need of a complete dictionary of the English language, the birth of a Littré, who would devote his life to this work, was not waited for. Volunteers were appealed to, and a thousand men offered their services, spontaneously and gratuitously, to ransack the libraries, to take notes, and to accomplish in a few years a work which one man could not complete in his lifetime. In all branches of human intelligence the same spirit is breaking forth, and we should have a very limited knowledge of humanity could we not guess that the future is announcing itself in such tentative co-operation, which is gradually taking the place of individual work.

For this dictionary to be a really collective work, it would have required that many volunteer authors, printers and printers' readers should have worked in common; but something in this direction is done already in the Socialist Press, which offers us examples of manual and intellectual work combined. It happens in our newspapers that a Socialist author composes in lead his own article. True, such attempts are rare, but they indicate in which direction evolution is going.

They show the road of liberty. In future, when a man will have something useful to say-a word that goes beyond the thoughts of his century, he will not have to look for an editor who might advance the necessary capital. He will look for collaborators among those who know the printing trade, and who approve the idea of his new work. Together they will publish the new book or journal.

Literature and journalism will cease to be a means of money-making and living at the cost of others. But is there any one who knows literature and journalism from within, and who does not ardently desire that literature should at last be able to free itself from those who formerly protected it, and who now exploit it, and from the multitude which with rare exceptions pays it in proportion to its mediocrity, or to the ease with which it adapts itself to the bad taste of the greater number?

Letters and science will only take their proper place in the work of human development when, freed from all mercenary bondage, they will be exclusively cultivated by those that love them, and for those that love them.

IV

Literature, science, and art must be cultivated by free men. Only on this condition will they succeed in emancipating themselves from the yoke of the State, of Capital, and of the bourgeois mediocrity which stifles them.

What means has the scientist of to-day to make researches that interest him? Should he ask help of the State, which can only be given to one candidate in a hundred, and which none may obtain who does not ostensibly promise to keep to the beaten track? Let us remember how the Institute of France censured Darwin how the Academy of St. Petersburg treated Mendeléeff with contempt, and how the Royal Society of London refused to publish Joule's paper, in which he determined the mechanical equivalent of heat, finding it "unscientific."*

It is why all great researches, all discoveries revolutionizing science, have been made outside academies and universities, either by men rich enough to remain independent, like Darwin and Lyell, or by men who undermined their health by working in poverty and often in great straits, losing no end of time

* We know this from Playfair, who mentioned it at Joule's death.

for want of a laboratory, and unable to procure the instruments or books necessary to continue their researches, but persevering against hope and often dying before they had reached the end in view Their name is legion.

Altogether, the system of help granted by the State is so bad that science has always endeavoured to emancipate itself from it. For this very reason there are thousands of learned societies organized and maintained by volunteers in Europe and America,—some having developed to such a degree that all the resources of subventioned societies, and the wealth of millionaires would not buy their treasures. No governmental institution is as rich as the Zoological Society of London, which is supported by voluntary contributions.

It does not buy the animals which in thousands people its gardens: they are sent by other societies and by collectors of the entire world. The Zoological Society of Bombay will send an elephant as a gift; another time a hippopotamus or a rhinoceros is offered by Egyptian naturalists.

And these magnificent presents are pouring in every day, arriving from all quarters of the globe—birds, reptiles, collections of insects, etc. These consignments often comprise animals that could not be bought for all the gold in the world; thus, a traveller who has captured an animal at life's peril, and now loves it as he would love a child, will give it to the Society because he is sure it will be cared for. The entrance fee paid by visitors and they are numberless, suffices for the maintenance of that immense institution.

What is defective in the Zoological Society of London, and in other kindred societies, is that the member's fee cannot be paid in work: that the keepers and numerous employés of this Large institution are not recognized as members of the Society, while many have no other incentive to joining the society than to put the cabalistic letters F.Z.S. (Fellow of the Zoological Society) on their cards. In a word, what is needed is a more perfect co-operation.

We may say the same about inventors that we have said of scientists. Who does not know what sufferings nearly all great inventions that have come to light have cost? Sleepless nights, families deprived of bread, want of tools and materials for experiments, is the history of nearly all those who have enriched industry with inventions which are the truly legitimate pride of our civilization.

But what are we to do to alter conditions that everybody is convinced are bad? Patents have been tried, and we know with what results. The inventor sells his patent for a few shillings, and the man who has only lent the capital pockets the often enormous profits resulting from the invention. Besides, patents isolate the inventor. They compel him to keep secret his researches which therefore end in failure; whereas the simplest suggestion, coming from a brain less absorbed in the fundamental idea, sometimes suffices to fertilize the invention and make it practical. Like all State control, patents hamper the progress of industry. Thought being incapable of being patented, patents are a crying injustice in theory, and in practice they result in one of the great obstacles to the rapid development of invention.

What is needed to promote the spirit of invention is, first of all, the awakening of thought, the boldness of conception, which our entire education causes to languish; it is the spreading of a scientific education, which would increase the number of inquirers a hundred-fold; it is faith that humanity is going to take a step forward, because it is enthusiasm, the hope of doing good, that has inspired all the great inventors. The Social Revolution alone can give this impulse to thought, this boldness, this knowledge, this conviction of working for all.

Then we shall have vast institutes supplied with motor-power and tools of all sorts, immense industrial laboratories open to all inquirers, where men will be able to work out their dreams, after having acquitted themselves of their duty towards society; where they will spend their five or six hours of leisure; where they will make their experiments; where they will find other comrades, experts in other branches of industry, likewise coming to study some difficult problem, and therefore able to help and enlighten each other, the encounter of their ideas and experience causing the longed-for solution to be found. And yet again, this is no dream. Solanoy Gorodok, in Petersburg, has already partially realized it as regards technical matters. It is a factory well furnished with tools and free to all; tools and motor-power are supplied gratis, only metals and wood are charged for at cost price. Unfortunately workmen only go there at night when worn out by ten hours' labour in the workshop. Moreover, they carefully hide their inventions from each other, as they are hampered by patents and Capitalism, that bane of present society, that stumbling-block in the path of intellectual and moral progress.

V

And what about art? From all sides we hear lamentations about the decedence of art. We are, indeed, far behind the great masters of the Renaissance. The technicalities of art have recently made great progress; thousands of people gifted w ith a certain amount of talent cultivate every branch, but art seems to fly from civilization! Technicalities make headway, but inspiration frequents artists' studios less than ever.

Where, indeed, should it come from? Only a grand idea can inspire art. Art is in our ideal synonymous with creation, it must look ahead; but save a few rare, very rare exceptions, the professional artist remains too philistine to perceive new horizons.

Moreover, this inspiration cannot come from books; it must be drawn from life, and present society cannot arouse it.

Raphael and Murillo painted at a time when the search of a new ideal could adapt itself to old religious traditions. They painted to decorate great churches which represented the pious work of several generations. The basilic with its mysterious aspect, its grandeur, was connected with the life itself of the city and could inspire a painter. He worked for a popular monument; he spoke to his fellow-citizens, and in return he received inspiration; he appealed to the multitude in the same way as did the nave, the pillars, the stained windows, the statues, and the carved doors. Nowadays the greatest honour a painter can aspire to is to see his canvas, framed in gilded wood, hung in a museum, a sort of old curiosity shop, where you see, as in the Prado, Murillo's Ascension next to a beggar of Velasquez and the dogs of Philip II. Poor Velasquez and poor Murillo! Poor Greek statues which *lived* in the Acropolis of their cities, and are now stifled beneath the red cloth hangings of the Louvre!

When a Greek sculptor chiselled his marble he endeavoured to express the spirit and heart of the city. All its passions, all its traditions of glory, were to live again in the work. But to-day the *united* city has ceased to exist; there is no more communion of ideas. The town is a chance agglomeration of people who do not know one another, who have no common interest, save the of enriching themselves at the expense of one another. The fatherland does not exist.... What fatherland can the international banker and the rag-picker have in common? Only when cities, territories, nations, or groups of nations, will have renewed their harmonious life, will art be able to draw its inspiration from *ideals held in common.* Then will the architect conceive the city's monument which will no longer be a temple, a prison, or a fortress; then will the painter, the sculptor, the carver, the ornament; worker know where to put their canvases, their statues, and their decorations; deriving their power of execution from the same vital source, and gloriously marching all together towards the future.

But till then art can only vegetate. The best canvases of modern artists are those that represent nature, villages, valleys, the sea with its dangers, the mountain with its splendours. But how can the painter express the poetry of work in the fields if he has only contemplated it, imagined it, if he has never delighted in it himself? If he only knows it as a bird of passage knows the country he soars over on his migrations? If, in the vigour of early youth, he has not followed the plough at dawn and enjoyed mowing grass with a large swathe of the scythe next to hardly haymakers vying in energy with lively young girls who fill the air with their songs? The love of the soil and of what grows on it is not acquired by sketching with a paint brush—it is only in its service; and without loving it, how paint it. This is why all that the best painters have produced in this direction is still so imperfect, not true to life, nearly always merely sentimental. There is no *strength* in it.

You must have seen a sunset when returning from work. You must have been a peasant among peasants to keep the splendour of it in your eye. You must have been at sea with fishermen at all hours of the day and night, have fished yourself, struggled with the waves faced the storm, and after rough work experienced the joy of hauling a heavy net, or the disappointment of seeing it empty, to understand the poetry of fishing. You must have spent time in a factory, known the fatigues and the joys of creative work, forged metals by the vivid light of a blast furnace, have felt the life in a machine, to understand the power of man and to express it in a work of art. You must in fact, be permeated with popular feelings, to describe them. Besides, the works of future artists who will have lived the life of the people, like the great artists of the past, will not be destined for sale. They will be an integrant part of a living whole that would not be complete without them, any more than they would be complete without it. Men will go to the artist's own city to gaze at his work, and the spirited and serene beauty of such creations will produce its beneficial effect on heart and mind.

Art, in order to develop, must be bound up with industry by a thousand intermediate degrees blended, so to say, as Ruskin and the great Socialist poet Morris have proved so often and so well. Everything that surrounds man, in the street, in the interior and exterior of public monuments, must be of a pure artistic form.

But this will only be capable of realization in a society in which all enjoy comfort and leisure. Then we shall see art associations, in which each can find room for his capacity, for art cannot dispense with an infinity of purely manual and technical supplementary works. These artistic associations will undertake to embellish the houses of their members, as those kind volunteers, the young painters of Edinburgh, did in decorating the walls and ceilings of the great hospital for the poor in their city.

A painter or sculptor who has produced a work of personal feeling will offer it to the woman he loves, or to a friend. Executed for love's sake, will his work, inspired by love, be inferior to the art that to-day satisfies the vanity of the philistine because it has cost much money?

Thc same will be done as regards all pleasure not comprised in the necessaries of life. He who wishes for a grand piano will enter the association of musical instrument makers. And by giving the association part of his half-days' leisure, he will soon possess the piano of his dreams. If he is passionately fond of astronomical studies he will join the association of astronomers, with it philosophers, its observers, its calculators, with its artists in astronomical instruments, its scientists and amateurs, and he will have the telescope he desires by taking his share of the associated work, for it is especially the rough work that is needed in an astronomical observatory bricklayer's, carpenter's, founder's, mechanic's work, the last touch being given to the instrument of precision by the artist.

In short, the five or seven hours a day which each will have at his disposal, after having consecrated several hours to the production of necessities, will amply suffice to satisfy all longings for luxury however varied. Thousands of associations would undertake to supply them. What is now the privilege of an insignificant minority would be accessible to all. Luxury, ceasing to be a foolish and ostentatious display of the bourgeois class, would become an artistic pleasure.

Every one would be the happier for it. In collective work, performed with a light heart to attain a desired end, a book, a work of art, or an object of luxury, each will find an incentive, and the necessary relaxation that makes life pleasant.

In working to put an end to the division between master and slave we work for the happiness of both, for the happiness of humanity.

CHAPTER-X

AGREEABLE WORK

I

When Socialists declare that a society, emancipated from Capital, would make work agreeable, and would suppress all repugnant and unhealthy drudgery, they get laughed at. And yet even to-day we can see the striking progress made in this direction; and wherever this progress has been achieved, employers congratulate themselves on the economy of energy obtained thereby.

It is evident that a factory could be made as healthy and pleasant as a scientific laboratory. And it is no less evident that it would be advantageous to make it so. In a spacious and well-ventilated factory work is better; it is easy to introduce small ameliorations, of which each represents an economy of time or of manual labour. And if most of the workshops we know are foul and unhealthy, it is because the workers are of no account in the organization of factories, and because the most absurd waste of human energy is its distinctive feature.

Nevertheless, now and again, we already find some factories so well managed that it would be a real pleasure to work in them, if the work, be it well understood, were not to last more than four or five hours a day, and if every one had the possibility of varying it according to his tastes.

Look at this factory, unfortunately consecrated to engines of war. It is perfect as far as regards sanitary and intelligent organization. It occupies fifty English acres of land, fifteen of which are roofed with glass. The pavement of fire-proof bricks is as clean as that of a miner's cottage, and the glass roof is carefully cleaned by a gang of workmen who do nothing else. In this factory are forged steel ingots or blooms weighing as much as twenty tons; and when you stand thirty feet from the immense furnace, whose flames have a temperature of more than a thousand degrees, you do not guess its presence save when its great jaws open to let out a steel monster. And the monster is handled by only three or four workmen, who now here, now there, open a tap, causing immense cranes to move by pressure of water in the pipes.

You enter expecting to hear the deafening noise of stampers, and you find that there are no stampers. The immense hundred-ton guns and the crank-shafts of transatlantic steamers are forged by hydraulic pressure, and instead of forging steel, the worker has but to turn a tap to give it shape, which makes a far more homogeneous metal, without crack or flaw, of the blooms, whatever be their thickness.

We expect an infernal grating, and we find machines which cut blocks of steel thirty feet long with no more noise than is needed to cut cheese. And when we expressed our admiration to the engineer who showed us round, he answered—

"It is a mere question of economy! This machine, that planes steel, has been in use for forty-two years. It would not have lasted ten years if its component parts, badly adjusted, lacking in cohesive strength, 'interfered' and creaked at each movement of the plane!"

"And the blast-furnaces? It would be a waste to let heat escape instead of utilizing it. Why roast the founders, when heat lost by radiation represents tons of coal?"

"The stampers that made buildings shake five leagues off were also waste! It is better to forge by pressure than by impact, and it costs less—there is less loss."

"In a factory, light, cleanliness, the space allotted to each bench, is but a simple question of economy. Work is better done when you can see and you have elbow-room."

"It is true,"; he said, "we were very cramped before coming here. Land is so expensive in the vicinity of large towns—landlords are so grasping!"

It is even so in mines. We know what mines are like nowadays from Zola's descriptions and from newspaper reports. But the mine of the future will be well ventilated, with a temperature as easily regulated as that of a library; there will be no horses doomed to die below the earth: underground traction will be carried on by means of an automatic cable put in motion at the pit's mouth. Ventilators will be always working, and there will never be explosions. This is no dream. Such a mine is already to be seen in England; we went down it. Here again this organization is simply a question of economy. The mine of which we speak, in spite of its immense depth (466 yards), has an output of a thousand tons of coal a day, with only two hundred miners—five tons a day per each worker, whereas the average for the two thousand pits in England is hardly three hundred tons a year per man.

If necessary, we could multiply examples proving that Fourier's dream regarding material organization was not a Utopia.

This question has, however, been so frequently discussed in Socialist newspapers that public opinion might have been educated. Factory, forge, and mine can be as healthy and magnificent as the finest laboratories in modern universities, and the better the organization the more will man's labour produce.

If it be so, can we doubt that work will become a pleasure and a relaxation in a society of equals, in which "hands" will not be compelled to sell themselves to toil, and to accept work under any conditions? Repugnant tasks will disappear, because it is evident that these unhealthy conditions are harmful to society as a whole. Slaves can submit to them, but free men will create new conditions, and their work will be pleasant and infinitely more productive. The exceptions of to-day will be the rule of to-morrow.

The same will come to pass as regards domestic work, which to-day society lays on the shoulders of that drudge of humanity—woman.

II

A society regenerated by the Revolution will make domestic slavery disappear—this last form of slavery, perhaps the most tenacious, because it is also the most ancient. Only it will not come about in the way dreamt of by Phalansterians, nor in the manner often imagined by authoritarian Communists.

Phalansteries are repugnant to millions of human beings. The most reserved man certainly feels the necessity of meeting his fellows for the purpose of common work, which becomes the more attractive the more he feels himself a part of an immense whole. But it is not so for the hours of leisure, reserved for rest and intimacy. The phalanstery and the familystery do not take this into account, or else they endeavour to supply this need by artificial groupings.

A phalanstery, which is in fact nothing but an immense hotel, can please some, and even all at a certain period of their life, but the great mass prefers family life (family life of the future, be it understood). They prefer isolated apartments, Normans and Anglo-Saxons even going as far as to prefer houses of from six to eight rooms, in which the family, or an agglomeration of friends, can live apart. Sometimes a phalanstery is a necessity, but it would be hateful, were it the general rule. Isolation, alternating with time spent in society, is the normal desire of human nature. This is why one of the greatest tortures in prison is the impossibility of isolation, much as solitary confinement becomes torture in its turn, when not alternated with hours of social life.

As to considerations of economy, which are sometimes laid stress on in favour of phalansteries, they are those of a petty tradesman. The most important economy, the only reasonable one, is to make life pleasant for all, because the man who is satisfied with his life produces infinitely more than the man who curses his surroundings.*

---

* It seems that the Communists of Young Icaria had understood the importance of a free choice in their daily relations apart from work. The ideal of religious Communists has

Other Socialists reject the phalanstery. But when you ask them how domestic work can be organized, they answer: "Each can do 'his own work.' My wife manages the house; the wives of bourgeois will do as much." And if it is a bourgeois playing at Socialism who speaks, he will add, with a gracious smile to his wife: "Is it not true, darling, that you would do without a servant in a Socialist society? You would work like the wife of our good comrade Paul or the wife of John the carpenter?"

Servant or wife, man always reckons on woman to do the house-work.

But woman, too, at last claims her share- in the emancipation of humanity. She no longer wants to be the beast of burden of the house. She considers it sufficient work to give many years of her life to the rearing of her children. She no longer wants to be the cook, the mender, the sweeper of the house! And, owing to American women taking the lead in obtaining their claims, there is a general complaint of the dearth of women who will condescend to domestic work in the United States. My lady prefers art, politics, literature, or the gaming tables; as to the work-girls, they are few, those who consent to submit to apron-slavery, and servants are only found with difficulty in the States. Consequently, the solution, a very simple one, is pointed out by life itself. Machinery undertakes three-quarters of the household cares.

You black your boots, and you know how ridiculous this work is. What can be more stupid than rubbing a boot twenty or thirty times with a brush? A tenth of the European population must be compelled to sell itself in exchange for a miserable shelter and insufficient food, and woman must consider herself a slave, in order that millions of her sex should go through this performance every morning.

But hairdressers have already machines for brushing glossy or woolly heads of hair. Why should we not apply, then, the same principle to the other extremity? So it has been done, and nowadays the machine for blacking boots is in general use in big American and European hotels. Its use is spreading outside hotels. In large English schools, where the pupils are boarding in the houses of the teachers, it has been found easier to have one single establishment which undertakes to brush a thousand pairs of boots every morning.

As to washing up! Where can we find a housewife who has not a horror of this long and dirty work, that is usually done by hand, solely because the work of the domestic slave is of no account.

---

always been to have meals in common ; it is by meals in common that early Christians manifested their adhesion to Christianity. Communion is still a vestige of it. Young Icarians had given up this rehgious tradition. They dined in a common dining-room, but at small separate tables, at which they sat according to the attractions of the moment. The Communists of Anama have each their house and dine at home, while taking their provisions at will at the communal stores

In America they do better. There are already a number of cities in which hot water is conveyed to the houses as cold water is in Europe. Under these conditions the problem was a simple one, and a woman—Mrs. Cochrane—solved it. Her machine washes twelve dozen plates or dishes, wipes them and dries them, in less than three minutes. A factory in Illinois manufactures these machines and sells them at a price within reach of the average middle-class purse. And why should not small households send their crockery to an establishment as well as their boots? It is even probable that the two functions, brushing and washing up, will be undertaken by the same association.

Cleaning, rubbing the skin off your hands when washing and wringing linen; sweeping floors and brushing carpets, thereby raising clouds of dust which afterwards occasion much trouble to dislodge from the places where they have settled down, all this work is still done because woman remains a slave, but it tends to disappear as it can be infinitely better done by machinery. Machines of all kinds will be introduced into households, and the distribution of motor-power in private houses will enable people to work them without muscular effort.

Such machines cost little to manufacture. If we still pay very much for them, it is because they are not in general use, and chiefly because an exorbitant tax is levied upon every machine by the gentlemen who wish to live in grand style and who have speculated on land, raw material, manufacture, sale, patents, and duties.

But emancipation from domestic toil will not be brought about by small machines only. Households are emerging from their present state of isolation; they begin to associate with other households to do in common what they did separately.

In fact, in the future we shall not have a brushing machine, a machine for washing up plates, a third for washing linen, and so on, in each house. To the future, on the contrary, belongs the common heating apparatus that sends heat into each room of a whole district and spares the lighting of fires. It is already so in a few American cities. A great central furnace supplies all houses and all rooms with hot water, which circulates in pipes; and to regulate the temperature you need only turn a tap. And should you care to have a blazing fire in any particular room you can light the gas specially supplied for heating purposes from a central reservoir. All the immense work of cleaning chimneys and keeping up fires—and woman knows what time it takes—is disappearing.

Candles, lamps, and even gas have had their day. There are entire cities in which it is sufficient to press a button for light to burst forth, and, indeed, it is a simple question of economy and of knowledge to give yourself the luxury of electric light. And lastly, also in America, they speak of forming societies for the almost complete suppression of household work. It would only be necessary to create a department for every block of houses. A cart would come to each door and take the boots to be blacked, the crockery to be washed up, the linen to be washed, the small things to be mended (if it were worth while), the carpets to be brushed, and the next morning would bring back the things entrusted to it all well cleaned. A few hours later your hot coffee and your eggs done to a nicety would appear on your table. It is a fact that between twelve and two o'clock there are more than twenty million Americans and as many Englishmen who eat roast beef or mutton, boiled pork, potatoes, and a seasonable vegetable. And at the lowest figure eight million fires burn during two or three hours to roast this meat and cook these vegetables; eight million women spend their time to prepare this meal, that perhaps consists at most of ten different dishes.

"Fifty fires burn," wrote an American woman the other day, "where one would suffice!" Dine at home, at your own table, with your children, if you like; but only think yourself, why should these fifty women waste their whole morning to prepare a few cups of coffee and a simple meal! Why fifty fires, when two people and one single fire would suffice to cook all these pieces of meat and all these vegetables? Choose your own beef or mutton to be roasted if you are particular. Season the vegetables to your taste if you prefer a particular sauce! But have a single kitchen with a single fire, and organize it as beautifully as you are able to.

Why has woman's work never been of any account? Why in every family are the mother and three or four servants obliged to spend so much time at what pertains to cooking? Because those who want to emancipate mankind have not included woman in their dream of emancipation, and consider it beneath their superior masculine dignity to think "of those kitchen arrangements," which they have rayed on the shoulders of that drudge- woman.

To emancipate woman is not only to open the gates of the university, the law courts, or the parliaments, for her, for the "emancipated" woman will always throw domestic toil on to another woman. To emancipate woman is to free her from the brutalizing toil of kitchen and washhouse; it is to organize your household in such a way as to enable her to rear her children, if she be so minded, while still retaining sufficient leisure to take her share of social life.

It will come to pass. As we have said, things are already improving. Only let us fully understand that a revolution, intoxicated with the beautiful words Liberty, Equality, Solidarity would not be a revolution if it maintained slavery at home. Half humanity subjected to the slavery of the hearth would still have to rebel against the other half.

CHAPTER-XI

FREE AGREEMENT

I

Accustomed as we are by hereditary prejudices and absolutely unsound education and training to see Government, legislation and magistracy everywhere around, we have come to believe that man would tear his fellow man to pieces like a wild beast the day the police took his eye off him; that chaos would come about if authority were overthrown during a revolution. And with our eyes shut we pass by thousands and thousands of human groupings which form themselves freely, without any intervention of the law, and attain results infinitely superior to those achieved under governmental tutelage.

If you open a daily paper you find its pages are entirely devoted to Government transactions and to political jobbery. A Chinaman reading it would believe that in Europe nothing gets done save by order of some master. You find nothing in them about institutions that spring up, grow up, and develop without ministerial prescription. Nothing - or hardly nothing! Even when there is a heading- Ã¬Sundry Events "- it is because they are connected with the police. A family drama, an act of rebellion, will only be mentioned if the police have appeared on the scene.

Three hundred and fifty million Europeans love or hate one another, work, or live on their incomes; but, apart from literature, theatre, or sport, their lives remain ignored by newspapers if Governments have not intervened in some way or other. It is even so with history. We know the least details of the life of a king or of a parliament; all good and bad speeches pronounced by the politicians have been preserved. "Speeches that have never had the least influence on the vote of a single member," as an old parliamentarian said. Royal visits, good or bad humour of politicians, jokes or intrigues, are all carefully recorded for posterity. But we have the greatest difficulty to reconstitute a city of the Middle Ages, to understand the mechanism of that immense commerce that was carried on between Hanseatic cities, or to know how the city of Rouen built its cathedral. If a scholar spends his life in studying these questions, his works remain unknown, and parliamentary histories- that is to say, the defective ones, as they only treat of one side of social life- multiply, are circulated, are taught in schools.

And we do not even perceive the prodigious work accomplished every day by spontaneous groups of men, which constitutes the chief work of our century.

We therefore propose to point out some of these most striking manifestations, and to prove that men, as soon as their interests do not absolutely clash, act in concert, harmoniously, and perform collective work of a very complex nature.

It is evident that in present society, based on individual property- that is to say, on plunder, and on a narrow minded and therefore foolish individualism- facts of this kind are necessarily few in number; agreements are not always perfectly free, and often have a mean, if not execrable aim.

But what concerns us is not to give examples which we could blindly follow, and which, moreover, present society could not possibly give us. What we have to do is to prove that, in spite of the authoritarian individualism which stifles us, there remains in our life, taken as a whole, a great part in which we only act by free agreement, and that it would be much easier than we think to dispense with Government.

In support of our view we have already mentioned railways, and we are about to return to them.

We know that Europe has a system of railways, 175,000 miles long, and that on this network you can nowadays travel from north to south, from east to west, from Madrid to Petersburg, and from Calais to Constantinople, without stoppages, without even changing carriages (when you travel by express). More than that: a parcel thrown into a station will find its addressee anywhere, in Turkey or in Central Asia, without more formality needed for sending it than writing its destination on a bit of paper.

This result might have been obtained in two ways. A Napoleon, a Bismarck, or some potentate having conquered Europe, would from Paris, Berlin, or Rome, draw a railway map and regulate the hours of the trains. The Russian Tsar Nicholas I dreamt of taking such action. When he was shown rough drafts of railways between Moscow and Petersburg, he seized a ruler and drew on the map of Russia a straight line between these two capitals, saying, Ã¬Here is the plan.Ã® And the road ad was built in a straight line, filling in deep ravines, building bridges of a giddy height, which had to be abandoned a few years later, at a cost of about £120,000 to £150,000 per English mile.

This is one way, but happily things were managed differently. Railways were constructed piece by piece, the pieces were joined together, and the hundred divers companies, to whom these pieces belonged, came to an understanding concerning the arrival and departure of their trains, and the running of carriages on their rails, from all countries, without unloading merchandise as it passes from one network to another.

All this was done by free agreement, by exchange of letters and proposals, by congresses at which relegates met to discuss certain special subjects, but not to make laws; after the congress, the delegates returned to their companies, not with a law, but with the draft of a contract to be accepted or rejected.

There were certainly obstinate men who would not he convinced. But a common interest compelled them to agree without invoking the help of armies against the refractory members.

This immense network of railways connected together, and the enormous traffic it has given rise to, no doubt constitutes the most striking trait of our century; and it is the result of free agreement. If a man had foreseen or predicted it fifty years ago, our grandfathers would have thought him idiotic or mad. They would have said: Ã¬Never will you be able to make the shareholders of a hundred companies listen to reason ! It is a Utopia, a fairy tale. A central Government, with an 'iron' director, can alone enforce it"

And the most interesting thing in this organization is, that there is no European Central Government of Railways! Nothing! No minister of railways, no dictator, not even a continental parliament, not even a directing committee! Everything is done by contract.

So we ask the believers in the State, who pretend that Ã¬we can never do without a central Government, were it only for regulating the traffic,Ã® we ask them: Ã¬But how do European railways manage without them? How do they continue to convey millions of travelers and mountains of luggage across a continent? If companies owning railways have been able to agree, why should railway workers, who would take possession of railways, not agree likewise? And if the Petersburg Warsaw Company and that of Paris Belfort can act in harmony, without giving themselves the luxury of a common commander, why, in the midst of our societies, consisting of groups of free workers, should we need a Government?

II

When we endeavour to prove by examples that even to-day, in spite of the iniquitous organization of society as a whole, men, provided their instincts be not diametrically opposed, agree without the intervention of authority, we do not ignore the objections that will be put forth.

These examples have their defective side, because it is impossible to quote a single organization exempt from the exploitation of the weak by the strong, the poor by the rich. That is why Statists will not fail to tell us with their wonted logic : " You see that the intervention of the State is necessary to put an end to this exploitation !"

Only they forget the lessons of history ; they do not tell us to what extent the State itself has contributed towards the existing order by creating proletarians and dehvering them up to exploiters. They also forget to tell us if it is possible to put an end to exploitation while the primal causes—private capital and poverty, two-thirds of which are artificially created by the State — continue to exist.

As regards the complete harmony among railway companies, we expect them to say : " Do you not see railway companies oppress and ill-use their employers and their travellers ! The State must intervene to protect the public !"

But have we not often repeated that as long as there are capitalists, this abuse of power will be perpetuated. It is precisely the State, the wouldbe benefactor, that has given to the companies that monopoly which they possess to-day. Has it not created concessions, guarantees ? Has it not sent its soldiers against railwaymen on strike ? And during the first trials (we see it in Russia), has it not extended the privilege to forbidding the Press mentioning railway accidents, so as not to depreciate the shares it guaranteed ? Has it not favoured the monopoly which has anointed the Vanderbilts and the Polyakoffs, the directors of the P.L.M., the C.P.R., the St. Gothard, " the kings of the times "

Therefore, if we give as an example the tacit agreement come to between railway companies, it is by no means as an ideal of economical management, nor even an ideal of technical organization. It is to show that if capitaHsts, without any other aim than that of augmenting their dividends at other people's expense, can exploit railways successfully without establishing an International Department, societies of working men will be able to do it just as well, and even better, without nominating a Ministry of European railways.

Another objection is raised that is more serious at first sight. We may be told that the agreement we speak of is not perfectly free, that the large companies lay down the law to the small ones. They might, for example, quote a certain rich company compelling travellers who go from Berlin to Bale to pass via Cologne and Frankfort, instead of taking the Leipzig route; a ?econd, carr5ring goods sixty or a hundred and thirty miles in a roundabout way (on long distances) to favour influential shareholders ; a third, ruining secondary lines. In the United States travellers and goods are sometimes compelled to travel impossibly circuitous routes so that dollars may flow into the pocket of a Vanderbilt.

Our answer will be the same : As long as Capital exists, the greater Capital will oppress the lesser. But oppression does not result from Capital only. It is also owing to the support given them by the State, to monopoly created by the State in their favour, that certain large companies oppress the little ones.

The early Socialists have shown how English legislation did all in its powers to ruin small industries, drive the peasant to poverty, and deliver over to wealthy industrial employers battahons of men, compelled to work for no matter what salary. Railway legislation did exactly the same. Strategic lines, subsidized lines, companies which received the International Mail monopoly, everything was brought into play to forward wealthy financiers' interests. When Rothschild, creditor to all European States, puts capital in a railway, his faithful subjects, the ministers, wiU do their best to make him earn more.

In the United States, in the Democracy that authoritarians hold up to us as an ideal, the most scandalous fraudulency has crept into everything that concerns railroads. Thus, if a company ruins its competitors by cheap fares, it is often enabled to do so because it is reimbursed by land given to it by the State for a gratuity. Documents recently published concerning the American wheat trade have fully shown up the part played by the State in the exploitation of the weak by the strong. Here, too, the power of accumulated capital has grown tenfold and a hundredfold by State help. So that, when we see syndicates of railway companies (a product of free agreement) succeeding in protecting their small companies against big ones, we are astonished at the intrinsic force of free agreement that can hold its own against aU-powerful Capital favoured by the State.

It is a fact that httle companies exist, in spite of the State's partiaUty. If in France, land of centralization, we only see five or six large companies, there are more than a hundred and ten in Great Britain who agree remarkably weU, and who are certainly better organized for the rapid transit of travellers and goods than the French and German companies.

Moreover, that is not the question. Large Capital, favoured by the State, can always, if it he to its advantage, crush the lesser one. What is of importance to us is this : The agreement between hundreds of companies to whom the railways of Europe belong, was established without intervention of a central government laying down the law to the divers societies ; it has subsisted by means of congresses composed of delegates, who discuss among themselves, and submit proposals, not laws, to their constituents. It is a new principle that differs completely from all governmental principle, monarchical or republican, absolute or parliamentarian. It is an innovation that has been timidly introduced into the customs of Europe, but has come to stay.

Ill

How often have we not read in the writings of State - loving Socialists :" Who, then, will undertake the regulation of canal traf&c in future society ?

Should it enter the mind of one of your Anarchist 'comrades' to put his barge across a canal and obstruct thousands of boats, who will force him to yield to reason ?"

Let us confess the supposition to be somewhat fanciful, yet it might be said, for instance: "Should a certain commune, or a group of communes, want to make their barges pass before others, they might perhaps block the canal in order to carry stones, while wheat, needed in another commune, would have to stand by. Who 'then, would regulate the barge traffic if not the Government ?"

But real Ufe has again demonstrated that Government can be very well dispensed with here as elsewhere. Free agreement, free organization, replace that noxious and costly system, and do better.

We know what canals mean to Holland. They are its highways. We also know how much traf&c there is on the canals. What is carried along our highroads and railroads is transported on canal-boats in Holland. There you could find cause to fight, to make your boats pass before others. There the Government might really interfere to keep the traf&c in order.

Yet it is not so. The Dutch settled matters in a more practical way, long ago, by founding a kind of guilds, or syndicates of boatmen. These were free associations sprung from the very needs of navigation. The right of way for the boats was adjusted by a certain registered order ; they followed one another in turn. None were allowed to get ahead of the others under pain of being excluded from the guild. None could station more than a certain number of days along the qnay, and if the owner found no goods to carry during that timej so much the worse for him ; he had to depart with his empty barge to leave room for newcomers. Obstruction was thus avoided, even though the competition between the private owners of the boats continued to exist. Were the latter suppressed, the agreement would have been only the more cordial. It is unnecessary to add that the shipowners could adhere or not to the syndicate. That was their business, but most of them elected to join it. Moreover, these syndicates offered such great advantages that they spread also along the Rhine, the Weser, the Oder, and as far as Berlin. The boatmen did not wait for a great Bismarck to annex Holland to Germany, and to appoint an Ober Haupt General Staats Canal Navigations Rath (Supreme Head Councillor of the General States Canal Navigation), with a number of stripes corresponding to the length of the title. They preferred coming to an international understanding. Besides, a number of shipowners, whose sailing-vessels ply between Germany and Scandinavia, as well as Russia, have also joined these syndicates, in order to regulate traffic in the Baltic and to bring about a certain harmony in the chasse-crois^ of vessels. These associations have sprung up freely, recruiting volunteer adherents, and have nought in common with governments.

It is, however, more than probable that here too greater capital oppresses lesser. Maybe the syndicate has also a tendency to become a mono poly, especially where it receives the precious patronage of the State that will not fail to interfere with it. Let us not forget either that these S5nidicates represent associations whose members have only private interests at stake, and that if at the same time each shipowner were compelled—by the socializing of production, consumption, and exchange—to belong to a hundred other associations for the satisfying of his needs, things would have a different aspect. A group of shipowners, powerful on sea, would feel weak on land, and they would be obhged to lessen their claims in order to come to terms with railways, factories, and other groups.

At any rate, without discussing the future, here is another spontaneous association that has dispensed with Government. Let us quote more examples.

As we are talking of ships and boats, let us mention one of the most splendid organizations that our century has brought forth, one of those we may with right be proud of—the English Lifeboat Association.

It is known that every year more than a thousand ships are wrecked on the shores of England. At sea a good ship seldom fears a storm. It is near the coasts that danger threatens—rough seas that shatter her stern-post, squalls that carry off her masts and sails, currents that render her unmanageable, reefs and sand banks on which she runs aground.

Even in olden times, when it was a custom among inhabitants of the coasts to Hght fires in order to attract vessels on to reefs, and to seize their cargoes, they always strove to save the crew. Seeing a ship in distress, they launched their nutshells and went to the rescue of shipwrecked sailors, only too often finding a watery grave themselves. Every hamlet along the seashore has its legends of heroism, displayed by woman as well as by man, to save crews in distress.

No doubt the State and men of science have done something to diminish the number of casualties. Lighthouses, signals, charts, meteorological warnings have diminished them greatly, but there remain a thousand ships and several thousand human hves to be saved every year.

To this end a few men of goodwill put their shoulders to the wheel. Being good sailors and navigators themselves, they invented a lifeboat that could weather a storm without being torn to pieces or capsizing, and they set to work to interest the public in their venture, to collect the necessary funds for constructing boats, and for stationing them along the coasts, wherever they could be of use.

These men, not being Jacobins, did not turn to the Government. They understood that to bring their enterprise to a successful issue they must have the co-operation, the enthusiasm, the local knowledge, and especially the self-sacrifice of sailors. They also understood that to find men who at the first signal would launch their boat at night, in a chaos of waves, not suffering

themselves to be deterred by darkness or breakers, and struggling five, six, ten hours against the tide before reaching a vessel in distress—men ready to risk their lives to save those of others, there must be a feeling of solidarity, a spirit of sacrifice not to be bought with galloon. It was therefore a perfectly spontaneous movement, sprung from agreement and individual initiative. Hundreds of local groups arose along the coasts. The initiators had the common sense not to pose as masters. They looked for sagacity in the fishermen's hamlets, and when a lord sent ;£iooo to a village on the coast to erect a lifeboat station, and his offer was accepted, he left the choice of a site to the local fishermen and sailors.

, Models of new boats were not submitted to the Admiralty. We read in a Report of the Association : " As it is of importance that hfeboatmen should have full confidence in the vessel they man, the Committee will make a point of constructing and equipping the boats according to the hfeboatmen's expressed wish." In consequence every year brings with it new improvements.

The work is wholly conducted by volunteers organizing in committees and local groups ; by mutual aid and agreement !—Oh, Anarchists !— Moreover, they ask nothing of ratepayers, and in a year they may receive £40,000 in spontaneous subscriptions.

As to the results, here they are : In 1891 the Association possessed 293 hfeboats. The same year it saved 601 shipwrecked sailors and 33 vessels. Since its foundation it has saved 32,671 human beings.

In 1886, three lifeboats with all their men having perished at sea, hundreds of new volunteers entered their names, organized themselves into local groups, and the agitation resulted in the construction of twenty additional boats. As we proceed, let us note that every year the Association sends to the fishermen and sailors excellent barometers, at a price three times less than their sale price. It propagates meteorological knowledge, and warns the parties concerned of the sudden changes predicted by men of science.

Let us repeat that these hundreds of committees and local groups are not organized hierarchically, and are composed exclusively of volunteers, hfeboatmen, and people interested in the work. The Central Committee, which is more of a centre for correspondence, in no wise interferes.

It is true that when voting on a question of education or local taxation takes place in a district, these committees do not, as such, take part in the deliberations, a modesty, which unfortunately the members of elected bodies do not imitate. But, on the other hand, these brave men do not allow those who have never faced a storm to legislate for them about saving life. At the first signal of distress they rush forth, concert, and go ahea,d. There are no galloons, but much goodwill.

Let us take another society of the same kind, that of the Red Cross. The name matters little; let us examine it.

Imagine somebody saying twenty -five years ago : " The State, capable as it is of massacring twenty thousand men in a day, and of wounding fifty thousand more, is incapable of helping its own victims ; as long as war exists private initiative must intervene, and men of goodwill must organize internationally for this humane work !" What mockery would not have met the man who would have dared thus to speak ! To begin with he would have been called Utopian, and if that did not silence him he would have been told: "Volunteers will be found wanting precisely where they are most needed, your hospitals will be centraUzed in a safe place, while what is indispensable will be wanting in the ambulances. National rivalry will cause poor soldiers to die without help." Disheartening remarks are only equalled by the number of speakers. Who of us has not heard men hold forth in this strain ?

Now we know what happened. Red Cross societies organized themselves freely, everywhere, in all countries, in thousands of localities; and when the war of 1870-1 broke out, the volunteers set to work. Men and women offered their services. Thousands of hospitals and ambulances were organized ; trains were started carrying ambulances, provisions, linen, and medicaments for the wounded. The English committees sent entire convoys of food, clothing, tools, grain to sow, beasts of draught, even steam-ploughs with their attendants to help in the tillage of departments devastated by the war! Only consult *La Croix Rouge,* by Gustave Moynier, and you will be really struck by the immensity of the work performed.

As to the prophets ever ready to deny other men's courage, good sense, and intelligence, and believing themselves to be the only ones capable of ruling the world with a rod, none of their predictions were realized. The devotion of the Red Cross volunteers was beyond all praise. They were only too glad to occupy the most dangerous posts ; and whereas the salaried doctors of the State fled with their staff when the Prussians approached, the Red Cross volunteers continued their work under fire, enduring the brutalities of Bismarck's and Napoleon's officers, lavishing their care on the wounded of all nationahties. Dutch, Italians, Swedes, Belgians, even Japanese and Chinese agreed remarkably well. They distributed their hospitals and their ambulances according to the needs of the occasion. They vied with one another especially in the hygiene of their hospitals. And there is many a Frenchman who still speaks with deep gratitude of the tender care he received from a Dutch or German volunteer in the Red Cross ambulances. But what is this to an authoritarian ? His ideal is the regiment doctor, salaried by the State. What does he care for the Red Cross and its hygienic hospitals, if the nurses be not functionaries ?

Here is then an organization, sprung up but yesterday, and which reckons its members by hundreds of thousands; possesses ambulances, hospital trains, elaborates new processes for treating wounds, and so on, and is due to the spontaneous initiative of a few devoted men.

Perhaps we shall be told that the State has something to do with this organization. Yes, States have laid hands on it to seize it. The directing committees are presided over by those whom flunkeys call princes of the blood. Emperors and queens lavishly patronize the national committees. But it is not to this patronage that the success of the organization is due. It is to the thousand local committees of each nation ; to the activity of individuals, to the devotion of all those who try to help the victims of war. And this devotion would be far greater if the State did not meddle with it.

In any case, it was not by the order of an International Directing Committee that Englishmen and Japanese, Swedes and Chinamen, bestirred themselves to send help to the wounded in 1871. It was not by order of an international ministry that hospitals rose on the invaded territory and that ambulances were carried on to the battlefield. It was by the initiative of volunteers from each country. Once on the spot, they did not get hold of one another by the hair as foreseen by Jacobins; they all set to work without distinction of nationality.

We may regret that such great efforts should be put to the service of so bad. a cause, and ask ourselves hke the poet's child : " Why inflict wounds if you are to heal them afterwards ?" In striving to destroy the power of capital and bourgeois authority, we work to put an end to massacres, and we would far rather see the Red Cross volunteers put forth their activity to bring about (with us) the suppression of war; but we had to mention this immense organization as another illustration of results produced by free agreement and free aid.

If we wished to multiply examples taken from the art of exterminating men we should never end. Suffice to quote the numerous societies to which the German army owes its force, that does not only depend on discipline, as is generally believed. I mean the societies whose aim is to propagate military knowledge.

At one of the last congresses of the Military AUiance (Kriegerbund), delegates from 2452 federated societies, comprising 151,712 members, were present. But there are besides very numerous Shooting, Military Games, Strategical Games, Topographical Studies Societies—these are the workshops in which the technical knowledge of the German army is developed, not in regimental schools. It is a formidable network of all kinds of societies, including military men and civilians, geographers and gymnasts, sportsmen and technologists, which rise up spontaneously, organize, federate, discuss, and explore the country. It is these voluntary and free associations that make up the real backbone of the German army.

Their aim is execrable. It is the maintenance of the Empire. But what concerns us, is to point out that, in spite of military organization being the " Great mission" of the State, success in this branch is the more certain the more it is left to the free agreement of groups and to the free initiative of individuals.

Even in matters pertaining to war, free agreement is thus appealed to; and to further prove our assertion let us mention the three hundred thousand British volunteers, the British National Artillery Association, and the Society, now in course of organization, for the defence of England's coasts, as well as the appeals made to the commercial fleet, the BicycHsts' Corps, and the new organizations of private motor-cars and steam launches.

The State is abdicating and appeahng in its holy functions to private individuals. Everywhere free organization trespasses on its domain. And yet, the facts we have quoted let us catch only a glimpse of what free agreement has in store for us in the future, when there will be no more State.

CHAPTER-XII

OBJECTIONS

I

Let us now examine the principal objections put forth against Communism. Most of them are evidently caused by a simple misunderstanding, yet they raise important questions and merit our attention.

It is not for us to answer the objections raised by authoritarian Communism—we ourselves hold with them. Civilized nations have suffered too much in the long, hard struggle for the emancipation of the individual, to disown their past work and to tolerate a Government that would make itself felt in the smallest details of a citizen's life, even if that Government had no other aim than the good of the community. Should an authoritartan Socialist society ever succeed in establishing itself, it could not last; general discontent would soon force it to break up, or to reorganize itself on principles of liberty.

It is of an Anarchist-Communist society we are about to speak, a society that recognizes the absolute liberty of the individual, that does not admit of any authority, and makes use of no compulsion to drive men to work. Limiting our studies to the economic side of the question, let us see if such a society, composed of men as they are to-day, neither better nor worse, neither more nor less industrious, would have a chance of succssful development.

The objection is known. "If the existence of each is guaranteed, and if the necessity of earning wages does not compel men to work, nobody will work. Every man will lay the burden of his work on another if he is not forced to do it himself." Let us first remark the incredible levity with which this objection is raised, without taking into consideration that the question is in reality merely to know, on the one hand, whether you effectively obtain by wage-work the results you aim at; and, on the other hand, whether voluntary work is not already more productive to-day than work stimulated by wages. A question which would require profound study. But whereas in exact sciences men give their opinion on subjects infinitely less important and less complicated after serious research, after carefully collecting and analyzing facts, on this question they will pronounce judgment without appeal, resting satisfied with any one particular event, such as, for example, the want of success of a communist association in America. They act like the barrister, who does not see in the council for the opposite side a representative of a cause, or an opinion contrary to his own, but a simple adversary in an oratorical debate; and if he be lucky enough to find a repartee, does not otherwise care to justify his cause. Therefore the study of this essential basis of all Political Economy, the study of the most favourable conditions for giving society the greatest amount of useful products with the least waste of human energy, does not advance. They limit themselves to repeating commonplace assertions, or else they pretend ignorance of our assertions.

What is most striking in this levity is that even in capitalist Political Economy you already find a few writers compelled by facts to doubt the axiom put forth by the founders of their science, that the threat of hunger is man's best stimulant for productive work. They begin to perceive that in production a certain collective element is introduced which has been too much neglected up till now, and which might be more important than personal gain. The inferior quality of wage-work, the terrible waste of human energy in modern agricultural and industrial labour, the ever growing quantity of pleasure-seekers, who to-day load their burden on others' shoulders, the absence of a certain animation in production that is becoming more and more apparent; all this begins to preoccupy the economists of the "classical" school. Some of them ask themselves if they have not got on the wrong track: if the imaginary evil being, that was supposed to be tempted exclusively by a bait of lucre or wages, really exists. This heresy penetrates even into universities; it is found in books of orthodox economy.

This does not hinder a great many Socialist reformers to remain partisans of individual remuneration, and defending the old citadel of wagedom, notwithstanding that it is being delivered over stone by stone to the assailants by its former defenders.

They fear that without compulsion the masses will not work.

But during our own lifetime have we not heard the same fears expressed twice? By the anti-abolitionists in America before Negro emancipation, and by the Russian nobility before the liberation of the serfs? "Without the whip the Negro will not work," said the anti-abolitionist. "Free from their master's supervision the serfs will leave the fields uncultivated," said the Russian serf-owners. It was the refrain of the French noblemen in 1789, the refrain of the Middle Ages, a refrain as old as the world, and we shall hear it every time there is a question of sweeping away an injustice. And each time actual facts give it the lie. The liberated peasant of 1792 ploughed with a wild energy unknown to his ancestors, the emancipated Negro works more than his fathers, and the Russian peasant, after having honoured the honeymoon of his emancipation by celebrating Fridays as well as Sundays, has taken up work with as much eagerness as his liberation was the more complete. There, where the soil is his, he works desperately; that is the exact word for it. The anti-abolitionist refrain can be of value to slave-owners; as to the slaves themselves, they know what it is worth, as they know its motive.

Moreover, Who but economists taught us that if a wage-earner's work is but indifferent, an intense and productive work is only obtained from a man who sees his wealth increase in proportion to his efforts? All hymns sung in honour of private property can be reduced to this axiom.

For it is remarkable that when economists, wishing to celebrate the blessings of property, show us how an unproductive, marshy, or stony soil is clothed with rich harvests when cultivated by the peasant proprietor, they in nowise prove their thesis in favour of private property. By admitting: that the only guarantee not to be robbed of the fruits of your labour is to possess the instruments of labour—which is true—the economists only prove that man really produces most when he works in freedom, when he has a certain choice in his occupations, when he has no overseer to impede him, and lastly, when he sees his work bringing in a profit to him and to others who work like him, but bringing in nothing to idlers. This is all we can deduct from their argumentation, and we maintain the same ourselves.

As to the form of possession of the instruments of labour, they only mention it indirectly in their demonstration, as a guarantee to the cultivator that he shall not be robbed of the profits of his yield nor of his improvements. Besides, in support of their thesis in *favour of private property* against all other forms of *possession,* should not the economists demonstrate that under the form of communal property land never produces such rich harvests as when the possession is private? But it is not so; in fact, the contrary has been observed.

Take for example a commune in the canton of Vaud, in the winter time, when all the men of the village go to fell wood in the forest, which belongs to them all. It is precisely during these festivals of toil that the greatest ardour for work and the most considerable display of human energy are apparent. No salaried labour, no effort of a private owner can bear comparison with it.

Or let us take a Russian village, when all its inhabitants mow a field belonging to the commune, or farmed by it. There you will see what man can produce when he works in common for communal production. Comrades vie with one another in cutting the widest swath; women bestir themselves in their wake so as not to be distanced by the mowers. It is a festival of labour, in which a hundred people do work in a few hours that would not have been finished in a few days had they worked separately. What a sad contrast compared to the work of the isolated owner!

In fact, we might quote scores of examples among the pioneers of America, in Swiss, German, Russian, and in certain French villages; or the work done in Russia by gangs (artels) of masons, carpenters, boatmen, fishermen, etc., who undertake a task and divide the produce or the remuneration among themselves, without it passing through the intermediary of middlemen. We could also mention the great communal hunts of nomadic tribes, and an infinite number of successful collective enterprises. And in every case we could show the unquestionable superiority of communal work compared to that of the wage-earner or the isolated private owner.

Well-being, that is to say, the satisfaction of physical, artistic, and moral needs, has always been the most powerful stimulant to work. And when a hireling produces bare necessities with difficulty, a free worker, who sees ease and luxury increasing for him and for others in proportion to his efforts, spends infinitely far more energy and intelligence, and obtains first-class products in far greater abundance. The one feels riveted to misery, the other hopes for ease and luxury in the future. In this lies the whole secret. Therefore a society aiming at the well-being of all, and at the possibility of all enjoying life in all its manifestations, will supply voluntary work which will be infinitely superior and yield far more than work has produced up till now under the goad of slavery, serfdom, or wagedom.

II

Nowadays, whoever can load on others his share of labour indispensable to existence, does so, and it is admitted that it will always be so.

Now work indispensable to existence is essentially manual. We may be artists or scientists; but none of us can do without things obtained by manual work—bread, clothes, roads, ships, light, heat, etc. And, moreover, however highly artistic or however subtly metaphysical are our pleasures, they all depend on manual labour. And it is precisely this labour—basis of life—that every one tries to avoid.

We understand perfectly well that it must be so nowadays.

Because, to do manual work now, means in reality to shut yourself up for ten or twelve hours a day in an unhealthy workshop, and to remain riveted to the same task for twenty or thirty years, and maybe for your whole life.

It means to be doomed to a paltry wage, to the uncertainty of the morrow, to want of work, often to destitution, more often than not to death in a hospital, after having worked forty years to feed, clothe, amuse, and instruct others than yourself and your children.

It means to bear the stamp of inferiority all your life, because, whatever the politicians tell us, the manual worker is always considered inferior to the brain worker, and the one who has toiled ten hours in a workshop has not the time, and still less the means, to give himself the high delights of science and art, nor even to prepare himself to appreciate them; he must be content with the crumbs from the table of privileged persons.

We understand that under these conditions manual labour is considered a curse of fate.

We understand that all men have but one dream—that of emerging from, or enabling their cllildren to emerge from this inferior state; to create for themselves an "independent" position, which means what?—To also live by other men's work!

As long as there will be a class of manual workers and a class of "brain" workers, black hands and white hands, it will be thus.

What interest, in fact, can this depressing work have for the worker, when he knows that the fate awaiting him from the cradle to the grave will be to live in mediocrity, poverty, and insecurity of the morrow? Therefore, when we see the immense majority of men take up their wretched task every morning, we are surprised at their perseverance, at their zeal for work, at the habit that enables them, like machines blindly obeying an impetus given, to lead this life of misery without hope for the morrow; without foreseeing ever so vaguely that some day they, or at least their children, will be part of a humanity rich in all the treasures of a bountiful nature, in all the enjoyments of knowledge, scientific and artistic creation, reserved to-day to a few privileged favourites.

It is precisely to put an end to this separation between manual and brain work that we want to abolish wagedom, that we want the Social Revolution. Then work will no longer appear a curse of fate: it will become what it should be—the free exercise of *all* the faculties of man.

Moreover, it is time to submit to a serious analysis this legend about superior work, supposed to be obtained under the lash of wagedom

It is enough to visit, not the model factory and workshop that we find now and again, but ordinary factories, to conceive the immense waste of human energy that characterizes modern industry. For one factory more or less rationally organized, there are a hundred or more which waste man's labour, without a more substantial motive than that of perhaps bringing in a few pounds more per day to the employer.

Here you see youths from twenty to twenty five years of age, sitting all day long on a bench, their chests sunken in, feverishly shaking their heads and bodies to tie, with the speed of conjurers, the two ends of worthless scraps of cotton, the refuse of the lace-looms. What progeny will these trembling and rickety bodies bequeath to their country? "But they occupy so little room in the factory, and each of them brings me in sixpence a day," will say the employer.

In an immense London factory you could see girls, bald at seventeen from carrying trays of matches on their heads from one room to another, when the simplest machine could wheel the matches to their tables. But...it costs so little, the work of women who have no special trade! What is the use of a machine? When these can do no more, they will be easily replaced...there are so many in the street.

On the steps of a mansion on an icy night you will find a bare-footed child asleep, with its bundle of papers in its arms...child-labour costs so little that it may well be employed, every evening, to sell tenpenny-worth of papers, of which the poor boy will receive a penny, or a penny half-penny. And lastly, you may see a robust man tramping, dangling his arms; he has been out of work for months. Meanwhile his daughter grows pale in the overheated vapours of the workshop for dressing stuffs, and his son fills blacking pots by hand, or waits hours at the corner of a street till a passer-by enables him to earn a penny.

And so it is everywhere, from San Franeisco to Moscow, and from Naples to Stockholm. The waste of human energy is the distinguishing and predominant trait of industry, not to mention trade where it attains still more colossal proportions.

What a sad satire is that name, Political Economy, given to the science of waste of energy under the system of wagedom!

This is not all. If you speak to the director of a well-organized factory, he will naively explain to you that it is difficult nowadays to find a skilful, vigorous, and energetic workman, who works with a will. "Should such a man present himself among the twenty or thirty who call every Monday asking us for work, he is sure to be received, even if we are reducing the number of our hands. We recognize him at the first glance, and he is always accepted, even though we have to get rid of an older and less active worker the next day." And the one who has just received notice to quit, and all those who receive it to-morrow, go to reinforce that immense reserve army of capital—workmen out of work—who are only called to the loom or the bencd whcn there is pressure of work, or to oppose strikers. And those others, the average workers that are the refuse of the better-class factories? They join the equally formidable army of aged and indifferent workers that continually circulates between the second-class factories—those which barely cover their expenses and make their way in the world by trickery and snares laid for the buyer, and especially for the consumer in distant countries.

And if you talk to the workmen themselves, you will soon learn that the rule in such factories is—never to do entirely what you are capable of. "Shoddy pay—shoddy work!" this is the advice which the working man receives from his comrades upon entering such a factory.

For the workers know that if in a moment of generosity they give way to the entreaties of an employer and consent to intensify the work in order to carry out a pressing order, this nervous work will be exacted in the future as a rule in the scale of wages. Therefore in all such factories they prefer never to produce as much as they can. In certain industries production is limited so as to keep up high prices, and sometimes the password, "Go-canny," is given, which signifies, "Bad work for bad pay!"

Wage-work is serf-work; it cannot, it must not, produce all that it could produce. And it is high time to disbelieve the legend which represents wagedom as the best incentive to productive work. If inclustry nowadays brings in a hundred times more than it did in the days of our grandfathers, it is due to the sudden awakening of physical and chemical sciences towards the end of last century; not to the capitalist organization of wagedom, but in spite of that organization.

III

Those who have seriously studied the question do not deny any of the advantages of Communism, on condition, be it well understood, that Communism be perfectly free, that is to say, Anarchist. They recognize that work paid with money, even disguised under the name of "labour notes," to Workers' associations governed by the State, would keep up the characteristics of wagedom and would retain its disadvantages. They agree that the whole system would soon suffer from it, even if society came into possession of the instruments of production. And they admit that, thanks to integral education given to all chilclren, to the laborious habits of civilized societies, with the liberty of choosing and varying their occupations and the attractions of work done by equals for the well-being of all, a Communist society would not be wanting in producers who would soon make the fertility of the soil triple and tenfold, and give a new impulse to industry.

This our opponents agree to. "But the danger," they say, "will come from that minority of loafers who will not work, and will not have regular habits in spite of excellent conditions that make work pleasant. To-day the prospect of hunger compels the most refractory to move along with the others. The one who does not arrive in time is dismissed. But a black sheep suffices to contaminate the whole flock, and two or three sluggish or refractory workmen lead the others astray and bring a spirit of disorder and rebellion into the workshop that makes work impossible; so that in the end we shall have to return to a system of compulsion that forces the ringleaders back into the ranks. And is not the system of wages paid in proportion to work performed, the only one that enables compulsion to be employed, without hurting the feelings of the worker? Because all other means would imply the continual intervention of an authority that would be repugnant to free men." This, we believe, is the objection fairly stated.

It belongs to the category of arguments which try to justify the State, the Penal Law, the Judge, and the Gaoler.

"As there are people, a feeble minority, who will not submit to social customs," the authoritarians say, "we must maintain magistrates, tribunals and prisons, although these institutions become a source of new evils of all kinds."

Therefore we can only repeat what we have so often said concerning authority in general: "To avoid a possible evil you have recourse to means which in themselves are a greater evil, and become the source of those same abuses that you wish to remedy. For do not forget that it is wagedom, the impossibility of living otherwise than by selling your labour, which has created the present Capitalist system, whose vices you begin to recognize." Let us also remark that this authoritarian way of reasoning is but a justification of what is wrong in the present system. Wagedom was not instituted to remove the disadvantages of Communism; its origin, like that of the State and private ownership, is to be found elsewhere. It is born of slavery and serfdom imposed by force, and only wears a more modern garb. Thus the argument in favour of wagedom is as valueless as those by which they seek to apologize for private property and the State.

We are, nevertheless, going to examine the objection, and see if there is any truth in it.

To begin with, Is it not evident that if a society, founded on the principle of free work, were really menaced by loafers, it could protect itself without an authoritarian organization and without having recourse to wagedom?

Let us take a group of volunteers, combining for some particular enterprise. Having its success at heart, they all work with a will, save one of the associates, who is frequently absent from his post. Must they on his account dissolve the group, elect a president to impose fines, or maybe distribute markers for work done, as is customary in the Academy? It is evident that neither the one nor the other will be done, but that some day the comrade who imperils their enterprise will be told: "Friend, we should like to work with you; but as you are often absent from your post, and you do your work negligently, we must part. Go and find other comrades who will put up with your indifference!"

This way is so natural that it is practiced everywhere nowadays, in all industries, in competition with all possible systems of fines, docking of wages, supervison, etc.; a workman may enter the factory at the appointed time, but if he does his work badly, if he hinders his comrades by his laziness or other defects, and they quarrel with him on that account, there is an end of it; he is compelled to leave the workshop.

Authoritarians pretend that it is the almighty employer and his overseers who maintain regularity and quality of work in factories. In fact, in a somewhat complicated enterprise, in which the wares produced pass through many hands before being finished, it is the factory itself, the workmen as a unity, who see to the good quality of the work. Therefore the best factories of British private industry have few overseers, far less on an average than the French factories, and less than the British State factories.

A certain standard of public morals is maintained in the same way. Authoritarians say it is due to rural guards, judges, and policemen, whereas in reality it is maintained in spite of judges, policemen, and rural guards. "Many are the laws producing crimirials!" has been said long ago.

Not only in industrial workshops do things go on in this way; it happens everywhere, every day, on a scale that only bookworms have as yet no notion of. When a railway company, federated with other companies, fails to fulfil its engagements, when its trains are late and goods lie neglected at the stations, the other companies threaten to cancel the contract, and that threat usually suffices.

It is generally believed, at any rate it is taught, that commerce only keeps to its engagements from fear of lawsuits. Nothing of the sort; nine times in ten the trader who has not kept his word will not appear before a judge. There, where trade is very great, as in London, the sole fact of having driven a creditor to bring a lawsuit suffices for the immense majority of merchants to refuse for good to have any dealings with a man who has compelled one of them to go to law.

Then, why should means that are used to-day among mates in the workshop, traders, and railway companies, not be made use of in a society based on voluntary work?

Take, for example, an association stipulating that each of its members should carry out the following contract: "We undertake to give you the use of our houses, stores, streets, means of transport, schools, museums, etc., on condition that, from twenty to forty-five or fifty years of age, you consecrate four or five hours a day to some work recognized as necessary to existence. Choose yourself the producing groups which you wish to join, or organize a new group, provided that it will undertake to produce necessaries. And as for the remainder of your time, combine together with those you like for recreation, art, or science, according to the bent of your taste.

"Twelve or fifteen hundred hours of work a year, in a group producing food, clothes, or houses, or employed in public health, transport, etc., is all we ask of you. For this work we guarantee to you all that these groups produce or will produce. But if not one, of the thousands of groups of our federation, will receive you, whatever be their motive; if you are absolutely incapable of producing anything useful, or if you refuse to do it, then live like an isolated man or like an invalid. If we are rich enough to give you the necessaries of life we shall be delighted to give them to you. You are a man, and you have the right to live. But as you wish to live under special conditions, and leave the ranks, it is more than probable that you will suffer for it in your daily relations with other citizens. You will be looked upon as a ghost of bourgeois society, unless some friends of yours, discovering you to be a talent, kindly free you from all moral obligation towards society by doing necessary work for you.

"And lastly, if it does not please you, go and look for other conditions else where in the wide world, or else seek adherents and organize with them on novel principles. We prefer our own."

That is what could be done in a communal society in order to turn away sluggards if they became too numerous.

IV

We very much doubt that we need fear this contingency in a society really based on the entire freedom of the individual.

In fact, in spite of the premium on idleness offered by private ownership of capital, the really lazy man, unless he is ill, is comparatively rare.

Among workmen it is often said that bourgeois are idlers. There are certainly enough of them, but they, too, are the exception. On the contrary, in every industrial enterprise, you are sure to find one or more bourgeois who work very hard. It is true that the majority of bourgeois profit by their privileged position to award themselves the least unpleasant tasks, and that they work under hygienic conditions of air, food, etc., which permit them to do their business without too much fatigue. But these are precisely the conditions which we claim for all workers, without exception. We must also say that if, thanks to their privileged position, rich people often make absolutely useless or even harmful work in society, nevertheless the Ministers, Heads of Departments, factory owners, traders, bankers, etc., subject themselves for a few hours a day to work which they find more or less tiresome, all preferring their hours of leisure to this obligatory work. And if in nine cases out of ten this work is fateful, they find it none the less tiring for that. But it is precisely because the middle class put forth a great energy, even in doing harm (knowingly or not) and defending their privileged position, that they have succeeded in defeating the landed nobility, and that they continue to rule the masses. If they were idlers they would long since have ceased. to exist, and would have disappeared like the aristocrats. In a society that would expect only four or five hours a day of useful, pleasant, and hygienic work, they would perform their task perfectly, and they certainly would not put up with the horrible conditions in which men toil nowadays without reforming them. If a Huxley spent only five hours in the sewers of London, rest assured that he would have found the means of making them as sanitary as his physiological laboratory.

As to the laziness of the great majority of workers, only philistine economists and philanthropists say such nonsense.

If you ask an intelligent manufacturer, he will tell you that if workmen only put it into their heads to be lazy, all factories would have to be closed, for no measure of severity, no system of spying would be of any use. You should have seen the terror caused in 1887 among British employers when a few agitators started preaching the *"go-canny"* theory—"for bad pay bad work"; "take it easy, do not overwork yourselves, and waste all you can."—"They demoralize the worker, they want to kill industry!" cried those who formerly inveighed against the immorality of the worker and the bad quality of his work. But if the worker were what he is represented to be—namely, the idler whom you have continually to threaten with dismissal from the workshop—what would the word "demoralization" signify?

So when we speak of a possible idleness, we must well understand that it is a question of a small minority in society; and before legislating for that minority, would it not be wise to study its origin? Whoever observes with an intelligent eye sees well enough that the child reputed lazy at school is often the one which does not understand what he is badly taught. Very often, too, it is suffering from cerebral anÃ¦mia, caused by poverty and an anti-hygienic education. A boy who is lazy at Greek or Latin would work admirably were he taught in science, especially if taught by the medium of manual labour. A girl reputed nought at mathematics becomes the first mathematician of her class if she by chance meets somebody who can explain to her the elements of arithmetic she did not understand. And a workman, lazy in the workshop, cultivates his garden at dawn, while gazing at the rising sun, and will be at work again at nightfall, when all nature goes to its rest.

Somebody said that dirt is matter in the wrong place. The same definition applies to nine-tenths of those called lazy. They are people gone astray in a direction that does not answer to their temperament nor to their capacities. In reading the biography of great men, we are struck with the number of "idlers" among them. They were lazy as long as they had not found the right path, and afterwards laborious to excess. Darwin, Stephenson, and many others belonged to this category of idlers.

Very often the idler is but a man to whom it is repugnant to make all his life the eighteenth part of a pin, or the hundredth part of a watch, while he feels he has exuberant energy which he would like to expend elsewhere. Often, too, he is a rebel who cannot submit to being fixed all his life to a work-bench in order to procure a thousand pleasures for his emulover, while knowing himself to be far the less stupid of the two, and knowing his only fault to be that of having been born in hovel instead of coming into the world in a castle.

Lastly, a good many "idlers" do not know the trade by which they are compelled to earn their living. Seeing the imperfect thing made by their own hands, striving vainly to do better, and perceiving that they never will succeed on account of the bad habits of work already acquired, they begin to hate their trade, and, not knowing any other, hate work in general. Thousands of workmen and artists who are failures suffer from this cause.

On the other hand, he who since his youth has learned to play the piano well, to handle the plans *well,* the chisel, the brush, or the file, so that he feels that what he does is beautiful, will never give up the piano, the chisel, or the file. He *will* find pleasure in his work which does not tire him, as long as he is not overdriven.

Under the one name, *idleness,* a series of results due to different causes have been grouped, of which each one could be a source of good, instead of being a source of evil to society. Like all questions concerning criminality and related to human faculties, facts have been collected having nothing in common with one another. They say laziness or crime, without giving themselves the trouble to analyse their cause. They are in haste to punish them, without inquiring if the punishment itself does not contain a premium on "laziness" or "crime."*

This is why a free society, seeing the number of idlers increasing in its midst, would no doubt think of looking for the cause of laziness, in order to suppress it, before having recourse to punishment. When it is a case, as we have already mentioned, of simple bloodlessness, then, before stuffing the brain of a child with science, nourish his system so as to produce blood, strengthen him, and, that he shall not waste his time, take him to the country or to the seaside; there, teach him in the open air, not in books—geometry, by measuring the distance to a spire, or the height of a tree; natural sciences, while picking flowers and fishing in the sea; physical science, while building the boat he will go to fish in. But for mercy's sake do not fill his brain with sentences and dead languages. Do not make an idler of him!...

Such a child has neither order nor regular habits. Let first the children inculcate order among themselves, and later on, the laboratory, the workshop, work done in a limited space, with many tools about, will teach them method. But do not make disorderly beings out of them by your school, whose only order is the symmetry of its benches, and which—true image of the chaos in its teachings—will never inspire anybody with the love of harmony, of consistency, and method in work.

Do not you see that by your methods of teaching, framed by a Ministry for eight million scholars, who represent eight million different capacities,

* See my book, " In Russian and French Prisons." London, 1887.

you only impose a system good for mediocrities, conceived by an average of mediocrities? Your school becomes a University of laziness, as your prison is a University of crime. Make the school free, abolish your University grades, appeal to the volunteers of teaching; begin that way, instead of making laws against laziness which only serve to increase it.

Give the workman who is compelled to make a minute particle of some object, who is stifled at his little tapping machine, which he ends by loathing, give him the chance of tilling the soil, felling trees in the forest, sailing the seas in the teeth of a storm, dashing through space on an engine, but do not make an idler of him by forcing him all his life to attend to a small machine, to plough the head of a screw, or to drill the eye of a needle.

Suppress the cause of idleness, and you may take it for granted that few individuals will really hate work, especially voluntary work, and that there will be no need to manufacture a code of laws on their account.

CHAPTER-XIII

THE COLLECTIVIST WAGES SYSTEM

I

It is our opinion that collectivists commit a twofold error in their plans for the reconstruction of society. While speaking of abolishing capitalist rule, they intend nevertheless to retain two institutions which are the very basis of this rule—Representative Government and the Wages System.

As regards so-called representative government, we have often spoken about it. It is absolutely incomprehensible to us that intelligent men—and such are not wanting in the collectivist party—can remain partisans of national or municipal parliaments after all the lessons history has given them—in France, in England, in Germany, or in the United States.

While we see parliamentary rule breaking up, and from all sides criticism of this rule growing louder—not only of its results, but also of its principles—how is it that revolutionary socialists defend a system already condemned to die?

Built up by the middle classes to hold their own against royalty, sanctioning, and at the same time strengthening, their sway over the workers, parliamentary rule is pre-eminently a middle-class rule. The upholders of this system have never seriously affirmed that a parliament or a municipal council represent a nation or a city. The most intelligent among them know that this is impossible. The middle class has simply used the parliamentary system to raise a barrier between itself and royalty, without giving the people liberty. But gradually, as the people become conscious of their interests and the variety of their interests multiply, the system can no longer work. Therefore democrats of all countries vainly imagine (livers palliatives. The *Referendum* is tried and found to be a failure; proportional representation is spoken of, so is representation of minorities, and other parliamentary Utopias. In a word, they strive to find what is not to be found, and they are compelled to recognize that they are in a wrong way, and confidence in a Representative Government disappears.

It is the same with the wages system; for after having proclaimed the abolition of private property, and the possession in common of all means of production, how can they uphold the wages system in any form? It is, nevertheless, what collectivists are doing when they recommend *labour-cheques.*

It is easy to understand why the early English socialists came to the system of labour-cheques. They simply tried to make Capital and Labour agree. They repudiated the idea of violently laying hands on capitalist property.

It is also easily understood why Proudhon took up the idea later on. In his Mutualist system he tried to make Capital less offensive, notwithstanding the retaining of private property, which he detested from the bottom of his heart, but which he believed to be necessary to guarantee individuals against the State.

Neither is it astonishing that certain economists, more or less bourgeois, admit labour-cheques. They care little whether the worker is paid in labour-notes or in coin stamped with the effigy of the Republic or the Empire. They only care to save from destruction individual ownership of dwelling-houses, of land, of factories; in any case that of dwelling-houses and the capital that is necessary for manufacturing. And labour-notes would just answer the purpose of upholding this private property.

As long as labour-notes can be exchanged for Jewels or carriages, the owner of the house will willingly accept them for rent. And as long as dwelling-houses, fields, and factories belong to isolated owners, men will have to pay them, in one way or another, for being allowed to work in the fields or factories, or for living in the houses. The owners will accept to be paid by the workers in gold, in paper-money, or in cheques exchangeable for all sorts of commodities. But how can we defend labour-notes, this new form of wagedom, when we admit that houses, fields, and factories will no longer be private property, and that they will belong to the commune or the nation?

II

Let us closely examine this system of remuneration for work done, preached by French, German, English, and Italian collectivists (Spanish anarchists, who still call themselves collectivists, imply by Collectivism the possession in common of all instruments of production, and the "liberty of each group to divide the produce, as they think fit, according to communist or any other principles"). It amounts to this: Everybody works in field, factory, school, hospital, etc. The working-day is fixed by the State, which owns land, factories, roads, etc. Every work-day is paid for with a labour-note, which is inscribed with these words: Eight hours work. With this cheque the worker can procure all sorts of merchandise in the stores owned by the State or by divers corporations. The cheque is divisible, so that you can buy an hour's-work worth of meat, ten minutes worth of matches, or half an hour of tobacco. After the Collectivist Revolution, instead of saying "two-pence worth of soap," we shall say "five minutes worth of soap."

Most collectivists, true to the distinction laid down by middle-class economists (and by Marx) between *qualified* work and *simple* work, tell us, moreover, that qualified or professional work must be paid a certain quantity more than simple work. Thus an hour's work of a doctor will have to be considered as equivalent to two or three hours' work of a hospital nurse, or to three hours' work of a navvy. "Professional, or qualified work, will be a multiple of simple work," says the collectivist Gronlund, "because this kind of work needs a more or less long apprenticeship."

Other collectivists, such as the French Marxists, do not make this distinction. They proclaim "Equality of Wages." The doctor, the schoolmaster, and the professor will be paid (in labour-cheques) at the same rate as the navvy. Eight hours visiting the sick in a hospital will be worth the same as eight hours spent in earth-works or else in mines or factories.

Some make a greater concession; they admit that disagreeable or unhealthy work—such as sewerage—could be paid for at a higher rate than agreeable work. One hour's work of a sewerman would be worth, they say, two hours of a professor's work.

Let us add that certain collectivists admit of corporations paying a lump sum for work done. Thus a corporation would say: "Here are a hundred tons of steel. A hundred workmen were required to produce them, and it took them ten days. Their work-day being an eight-hours day, it has taken them eight thousand working hours to produce a hundred tons of steed eight hours a ton." For this the State would pay them eight thousand labour-notes of one hour each, and these eight thousand cheques would be divided among the members of the iron-works as they themselves thought proper.

On the other hand, a hundred miners having taken twenty days to extract eight thousand tons of coal, coal would be worth two hours a ton, and the sixteen thousand cheques of one hour each, received by the Guild of Miners, would be divided among their members according to their own appreciation.

If the miners protested, and said that a ton of steel should only cost six hours' work instead of eight; if the professor wished to have his day paid twice more than the nurse, then the State would interfere and would settle their differences.

Such is, in a few words, the organization collectivists wish to see arise out of the Social Revolution. As we see, their principles are: Collective property of the instruments of production, and remuneration to each according to the time spent in producing, while taking into account the productivity of his labour. As to the political system, it would be Parliamentarianism modified by *positive instructions* given to those elected, by the *Referendum*—a vote, taken by noes or ayes by the nation.

Let us own that this system appears to us unrealizable.

Collectivists begin by proclaiming a revolutionary principle—the abolition of private property—then they deny it no sooner than proclaimed by upholding an organization of production and consumption that originated in private property.

They proclaim a revolutionary principle, and ignore the consequences that this principle will inevitably bring about. They forget that the very fact of abolishing individual property in the instruments of work—land, factories, road, capital,—must launch society into absolutly new chanels; must completely overthrow the present system of production, both in its aim as well as in its means; must modify daily relations between individuals, as soon as land, machinery, and all other instruments of production are considered common property.

They say, "No private property," and immediately after strive to maintain private property in its daily manifestations. "You shall be a Commune as far as regards production: fields, tools, machinery, all that has been invented up till now—factories, railways, harbours, mines, etc., all are yours. Not the slightest distinction will be made concerning the share of each in this collective property.

"But from to-morrow you will minutely debate the share you are going to take in the creation of new machinery, in the digging of new mines. You will carefully weigh what part of the new produce belongs to you. You will count your minutes of work, and you will take care that a minute of your neighbours cannot buy more than yours.

"And as an hour measures nothing, as in some factories a worker can see to six power-looms at a time, while in another he only tends two, you will weigh the muscular force, the brain energy, and the nervous energy you have expended. You will accurately calculate the years of apprenticeship in order to appraise the amount each will contribute to future production. And this—after having declared that you do not take into account his share in past production."

Well, for us it is evident that a society cannot be based on two absolutely opposed principles, two principles that contradict one another continually. And a nation or a commune that would have such an organization would be compelled to revert to private property in the instruments of production, or to transform itself immediately into a communist society.

III

We have said that certain collectivist writers desire that a distinction should be made between qualified or professional work and simple work. They pretend that an hour's work of an engineer, an architect, or a doctor, must be considered as two or three hours' work of a blacksmith, a mason, or a hospital nurse. And the same distinction must be made between all sorts of trades necessitating a more or less long apprenticeship and the simple toil of day labourers.

Well, to establish this distinction would be to maintain all the inequalities of present society. It would mean fixing a dividing line, from the beginning, between the workers and those who pretend to govern them. It would mean dividing society into two very distinct classes—the aristocracy of knowledge above the horny-handed lower orders—the one doomed to serve the other; the one working with its hands to feed and clothe those who, profiting by their leisure, study how to govern their fosterers.

It would mean reviving one of the distinct peculiarities of present society and giving it the sanction of the Social Revolution. It would mean setting up as a principle an abuse already condemned in our ancient crumbling society.

We know the answer we shall get. They will speak of "Scientific Socialism"; they will quote bourgeois economists, and Marx too, to prove that a scale of wages has its raison d'Ãªtre, as "the labour-force" of the engineer will have cost more to society than the "labour-force" of the navvy. In fact,—have not economists tried to prove to us that if an engineer is paid twenty times more than a navvy it is because the "necessary" outlay to make an engineer is greater than that necessary to make a navvy? And has not Marx asserted that the same distinction is equally logical between two branches of manual labour? He could not conclude otherwise, having on his own account taken up Ricardo's theory of value, and upheld that goods are exchanged in proportion to the quantity of work socially necessary for their production.

But we know what to think of this. We know that if engineers, scientists, or doctors are paid ten or a hundred times more than a labourer, and that a weaver earns three times more than an agricultural labourer, and ten times more than a girl in a match factory, it is not by reason of their "cost of production," but by reason of a monopoly of education, or a monopoly of industry. Engineers, scientists, and doctors merely exploit their capital—their diplomas—as middle-class employers exploit a factory, or as nobles used to exploit their titles titles of nobility.

As to the employer who pays an engineer twenty times more than a labourer, it is simply due to personal interest; if the engineer can economize £4000 a year on the cost of production, the employer pays him £800 And if the employer has a foreman who saves £400 on the work by cleverly sweating workmen, he gladly gives him £80 or £120 a year. He parts with an extra £40 when he expects to gain £400 by it; and this is the essence of the Capitalist system. The same differences obtain among divers manual trades.

Let them, therefore, not talk to us of "the cost of production" which raises the cost of skilled labour, and tell us that a student who has gaily spent his youth in a university has a right to a wage ten times greater than the son of a miner who has grown pale in a mine since the age of eleven; or that a weaver has a right to a wage three or four times greater than that of an agricultural labourer. The cost of teaching a weaver his work is not four times greater than the cost of teaching a peasant his. The weaver simply benefits by the advantages his industry reaps in Europe, in comparison with countries that have as yet no industries.

Nobody has ever calculated the *cost of production* and if a loafer costs far more to society than a worker, it remains to be seen whether a robust day-labourer does not cost more to society than a skilled artisan, when we have taken into account infant-mortality among the poor, the ravages of anÃ¦mia, and premature deaths.

Could they, for example, make us believe that the 1s. 3d. paid to a Paris workwoman, the 3d. paid to an Auvergne peasant girl who grows blind at lace-making, or the 1s. 8d. paid to the peasant represent their "cost of production." We know full well that people work for less, but we also know that they do so exclusively because, thanks to our wonderful organization, they would die of hunger did they not accept these mock wages.

For us the scale of remuneration is a complex result of taxes, of governmental tutelage, of Capitalist monopoly. In a word, of State and Capital. Therefore, we say that all wages theories have been invented after the event to justify injustices at present existing, and that we need not take them into consideration.

Neither will they fail to tell us that the Collectivist scale of wages would be an improvement. "It would be better," so they say, "to see certain artisans receiving a wage two or three times higher than common labourers, than to see a minister receiving in a day what a workman cannot earn in a year. It would be a great step towards equality."

For us this step would be the reverse of progress. To make a distinction between simple and professional work in a new society would result in the Revolution sanctioning and recognizing as a principle a brutal fact we submit to nowadays, but that we nevertheless find unjust. It would mean imitating those gentlemen of the French Assembly who proclaimed August 4th, 1789, the abolition of feudal rights, but who on August 8th sanctioned these same rights by imposing dues on the peasants to compensate the noblemen, placing these dues under the protection of the Revolution. It would mean imitating the Russian Government, which proclaimed, at the time of the emancipation of the serfs, that the land should henceforth belong to the nobility, while formerly the lands were considered belonging to the serfs.

Or else, to take a better known example, when the Commune of 1871 decided to pay members of the Commune Council 12s. 6d. a day, while the Federates on the ramparts received only 1s. 3d., this decision was hailed as an act of superior democratic equality. In reality, the Commune only ratified the former inequality between functionary and soldier, Government and governed. Coming from an Opportunist Chamber of Deputies, such a decision would have appeared admirable, but the Commune doomed her revolutionary principles because she failed to put them into practice.

Under our existing social system, when a minister gets paid £4000 a year, while a workman must content himself with £40 or less; when a foreman is paid two or three times more than a workman, and among workmen there is every gradation, from 8s. a day down to the peasant girl's 3d.; we disapprove of the high salary of the minister as well as of the difference between the 8s. of the workman and the 3d. of the poor woman. And we say, "Down with the privileges of education, as well as with those of birth!" We are anarchists precisely because these privileges revolt us.

They revolt us already in this authoritarian society. Could we endure them in a society that began by proclaiming equality?

That is why some collectivists, understanding the impossibility of maintaining a scale of wages in a society inspired by the breath of the Revolution, hasten to proclaim equality of wage. But they meet with new difficulties, and their equality of wages becomes the same unrealizable Utopia as the scale of wages of other collectivists.

A society having taken possession of all social wealth, having boldly proclaimed the right of all to this wealth—whatever share they may have taken in producing it will be compelled to abandon any system of wages, whether in currency or labour-notes.

IV

The collectivists say, "To each according to his deeds"; or, in other terms, according to his share of services rendered to society. They think it expedient to put this principle into practice as soon as the Social Revolution will have made all instruments of production common property. But we think that if the Social Revolution had the misfortune of proclaiming such a principle, it would mean its necessary failure; it would mean leaving the social problem, which past centuries have burdened us with, unsolved. In fact, in a society like ours, in which the more a man works the less he is remunerated, this principle, at first sight, may appear to be a yearning for justice. But it is really only the perpetuation of past injustice. It was by virtue of this principle that wagedom began, to end in the glaring inequalities and all the abominations of present society; because, from the moment work done was appraised in currency or in any other form of wage; the day it was agreed upon that man would only receive the wage he could secure to himself, the whole history of State-aided Capitalist Society was as good as written; it germinated in this principle.

Shall we, then, return to our starting-point and go through the same evolution again ? Our theorists desire it, but fortunately it is impossible. The Revolution will be communist; if not, it will be drowned in blood, and have to be begun over again.

Services rendered to society, be they work in factory or field, or mental services, cannot be valued in money. There can be no exact measure of value (of what has been wrongly-termed exchange value), nor of use value, with regard to production. If two individuals work for the community five hours a day, year in year out, at different work which is equally agreeable to them, we may say that on the whole their labour is equivalent. But we cannot divide their work, and say that the result of any particular day, hour, or minute of work of the one is worth the result of a minute or hour of the other.

We may roughly say that the man who during his lifetime has deprived himself of leisure during ten hours a day has given far more to society than the one who has only deprived himself of leisure during five hours a day, or who has not deprived himself at all. But we cannot take what he has done during two hours and say that the yield is worth twice as much as the yield of another individual, working only one hour, and remunerate him in proportion. It would be disregarding all that is complex in industry, in agriculture, in the whole life of present society; it would be ignoring to what extent all individual work is the result of past and present labour of society as a whole. It would mean believing ourselves to be living in the Stone Age, whereas we are living in an age of steel.

If you enter a coal-mine you will see a man in charge of a huge machine that raises and lowers a cage. In his hand he holds a lever that stops and reverses the course of the machine; he lowers it and the cage turns back in the twinkling of an eye; he raises it, he lowers it again with a giddy swiftness. All attention, he follows with his eyes fixed on the wall an indicator that shows him On a small scale, at which point of the shaft the cage is at each second of its progress; as soon as the indicator has reached a certain level he suddenly stops the course of the cage, not a yard higher nor lower than the required spot. And no sooner have the colliers unloaded their coal-wagons, and pushed empty ones instead, than he reverses the lever and again sends the cage back into space.

During eight or ten consecutive hours he must pay the closest attention. Should his brain relax for a moment, the cage would inevitably strike against the gear, break its wheels, snap the rope, crush men, and obstruct work in the mine. Should he waste three seconds at each touch of the lever, in our modern perfected mines, the extraction would be reduced from twenty to fifty tons a day.

Is it he who is of greatest use in the mine? Or, is it perhaps the boy who signals to him from below to raise the cage? Is it the miner at the bottom of the shaft, who risks his life every instant, and who will some day be killed by fire-damp? Or is it the engineer, who would lose the layer of coal, and would cause the miners to dig on rock by a simple mistake in his calculations? And lastly, is it the mine owner who has put all his capital into the mine, and who has perhaps, contrary to expert advice asserted that excellent coal would be found there?

All the miners engaged in this mine contribute to the extraction of coal in proportion to their strength, their energy, their knowledge, their intelligence, and their skill. And we may say that all have the right to live, to satisfy their needs, and even their whims, when the necessaries of life have been secured for all. But how can we appraise their work?

And, moreover, Is the coal they have extracted their work? Is it not also the work of men who have built the railway leading to the mine and the roads that radiate from all its stations? Is it not also the work of those that have tilled and sown the fields, extracted iron, cut wood in the forests, built the machines that burn coal, and so on?

No distinction can be drawn between the work of each man. Measuring the work by its results leads us to absurdity; dividing and measuring them by hours spent on the work also leads us to absurdity. One thing remains: put the needs above the works, and first of all recognize the right to live, and later on, to the comforts of life, for all those who take their share in production.

But take any other branch of human activity—take the manifestations of life as a whole. Which one of us can claim the higher remuneration for his work? Is it the doctor who has found out the illness, or the nurse who has brought about recovery by her hygienic care? Is it the inventor of the first steam-engine, or the boy, who, one day getting tired of pulling the rope that formerly opened the valve to let steam enter under the piston, tied the rope to the lever of the machine, without suspecting that he had invented the essential mechanical part of all modern machinery—the automatic valve.

Is it the inventor of the locomotive, or the work man of Newcastle, who suggested replacing the stones formerly laid under the rails by wooden sleepers, as the stones, for want of elasticity, caused the trains to derail? Is it the engineer on the locomotive? The signalman who can stop trains? The switchman who transfers a train from one line to another?—To whom do we owe the transatlantic cable? Is it to the engineer who obstinately affirmed that the cable would transmit messages when learned electricians declared it to be impossible? Is it to Maury, the scientist, who advised that thick cables should be set aside for others as thin as canes? Or else to those volunteers, come from nobody knows where, who spent their days and nights on deck minutely examining every yard of the cable, and removed the nails that the stockholders of steamship companies stupidly caused to be driven into the non-conducting wrapper of the cable, so as to make it unserviceable.

And in a wider sphere, the true sphere of life, with its joys, its sufferings, and its accidents, can not each one of us recall some one who has rendered him so great a service that we should be indignant if its equivalent in coin were mentioned? The service may have been but a word, nothing but a word spoken at the right time, or else it may have been months and years of devotion, and are we going to appraise these "incalculable" services in "labour-notes"?

"The works of each!" But human society would not exist for more than two consecutive generations if every one did not give infinitely more than that for which he is paid in coin, in "cheques," or in civic rewards. The race would soon become extinct if mothers did not sacrifice their lives to take care of their children, if men did not give all the time, without demanding an equivalent, if men did not give just to those from whom they expect no reward.

If middle-class society is decaying, if we have got into a blind alley from which we cannot emerge without attacking past institutions with torch and hatchet, it is precisely because we have calculated too much. It is because we have let ourselves be influenced into giving only to receive. It is because we have aimed at turning society into a commercial company based on *debit* and *credit*.

Collectivists know this. They vaguely under stand that a society could not exist if it carried out the principle of "Each according to his deeds." They have a notion that *necessaries*—we do not speak of whims—the needs of the individual, do not always correspond to his *works*. Thus De Paepe tells us: "The principle—the eminently Individualist principle—would, however, be *tempered* by social intervention, for the education of children and young persons (including maintenance and lodging), and by the social organization for assisting the infirm and the sick, for retreats for aged workers, etc." They understand that a man of forty, father of three children, has other needs than young man of twenty. They know that the woman who suckles her infant and spends sleepless nights at its bedside, cannot do as much work as the man who has slept peacefully. They seem to take in that men and women, worn out maybe by dint of overwork for society, may be incapable of doing as much work as those who have spent their time leisurely and pocketed their "labour-notes" in the privileged career of State functionaries.

They are eager to temper their principle. They say: "Society will not fail to maintain and bring up its children; to help both aged and infirm. Without doubt *needs* will be the measure of the cost that society will burden itself with, to temper the principle of deeds."

Charity, charity, always Christian charity, organized by the State this time. They believe in improving asylums for foundlings, in effecting old-age and sick insurances—so as to *temper* their principle. But they cannot yet throw aside the idea of "wounding first and healing afterwards!"

Thus, after having denied Communism, after having laughed at their ease at the formula—"To each according to his needs" these great economists discover that they have forgotten something, the needs of the producers, which they now admit. Only it is for the State to estimate them, for the State to verify if the needs are not disproportionate to the work.

The State will dole out charity. Thence to the English poor-law and the workhouse is but a step.

There is but a degree, because even this stepmother of a society against whom we are in revolt has also been compelled to *temper* her individualist principles; she, too, has had to make concessions in a communist direction and under the same form of charity.

She, too, distributes halfpenny dinners to prevent the pillaging of her shops; builds hospital—often very bad ones, though sometimes splendid ones—to prevent the ravages of contagious diseases. She, too, after having paid the hours of labour, shelters the children of those she has wrecked. She takes their needs into consideration and doles out charity.

Poverty, we have said elsewhere, was the primary cause of wealth. It was poverty that created the first capitalist; because, before accumulating "surplus value," of which we hear so much, men had to be sufficiently destitute to consent to sell their labour, so as not to die of hunger. It was poverty that made capitalists. And if the number of poor rapidly increased during the Middle Ages, it was due to the invasions and wars that followed the founding of States, and to the increase of riches resulting from the exploitation of the East, that tore the bonds asunder which once united agrarian and urban communities, and taught them to proclaim the principle of wages, so dear to exploiters, instead of the solidarity they formerly practised.

And it is this principle that is to spring from a revolution which men dare to call by the name of Social Revolution, a name so clear to the starved, the oppressed, and the sufferers?

It can never be. For the day on which old institutions will fall under the proletarian axe, voices will cry out: "Bread, shelter, ease for all!" And those voices will be listened to; the people will say: "Let us begin by allaying our thirst for life, for happiness, for liberty, that we have never quenched. And when we shall have tasted of this joy we will set to work to demolish the last vestiges of middle-class rule, its morality drawn from account-books, its 'debit and credit' philosophy, its 'mine and yours' institutions. 'In demolishing we shall build,' as Proudhon said; and we shall build in the name of Communism and Anarchy."

CHAPTER-XIV

CONSUMPTION AND PRODUCTION

I

Looking at society and its political organization from a different standpoint than that of authoritarian schools- for we start from a free individual to reach a free society, instead of beginning by the State to come down to the individual- we follow the same method in economic questions. We study the needs of individuals, and the means by which they satisfy them, before discussing Production, Exchange, Taxation, Government, etc.

To begin with, the difference may appear trifling, but in reality it upsets official Political Economy.

If you open the works of any economist you will find that he begins with PRODUCTION, the analysis of means employed nowadays for the creation of wealth; division of labour, manufacture, machinery, accumulation of capital. From Adam Smith to Marx, all have proceeded along these lines. Only in the latter parts of their books do they treat of CONSUMPTION, that is to say, of the means necessary to satisfy the needs of individuals; and, moreover, they confine themselves to explaining how riches are divided among those who vie with one another for their possession.

Perhaps you will say this is logical. Before satisfying needs you must create the wherewithal to satisfy them. But before producing anything, must you not feel the need of it? Is it not necessity that first drove man to hunt, to raise cattle, to cultivate land, to make implements, and later on to invent machinery? Is it not the study of needs that should govern production? It would therefore be quite as logical to begin by considering needs and afterwards to discuss the means of production in order to satisfy these needs.

This is precisely what we mean to do.

But as soon as we look at it from this point of view, Political Economy entirely changes its aspect. It ceases to be a simple description of facts, and becomes a *science*. We can define it as: *The study of the needs of humanity,and the means of satisfying them with the least possible waste of human energy.* Its true name should be, Physiology of Society. It constitutes a parallel science to the physiology of plants and animals, which also is the study of the needs of plants and animals, and the most advantageous ways of satisfying them. In the series of social sciences, the economy of human societies takes the place, occupied in the series of biological sciences by the physiology of organic bodies.

We say, here are human beings, united in a society. All feel the need of living in healthy houses. The savage's hut no longer satisfies them; they require a more or less comfortable solid shelter. The question is, then: whether, man's capacity for production being given, every man can have a house of his own? and what is hindering him from having it?

And we are soon convinced that every family in Europe could perfectly well have a comfortable house, such as are built in England, in Belgium, or in Pullman City, or else an equivalent set of rooms. A certain number of days' work would suffice to build a pretty little airy house, well fitted up and lighted by gas.

But nine-tenths of Europeans have never possessed a healthy house, because at all times common people have had to work day after day to satisfy the needs of their rulers, and have never had the necessary leisure or money to build, or to have built, the home of their dreams. And they can have no houses, and will inhabit hovels as long as present conditions remain unchanged.

As you see, we proceed contrary to economists, who immortalize the so-called laws of production, and reckoning up the number of houses built every year, demonstrate by statistics, that the new built houses not sufficing to meet all demands, nine-tenths of Europeans *must* live in hovels.

Let us pass on to food. After having enumerated the benefits accruing from the division of labour economists tell us the division of labour requires that some men should work at agriculture and others at manufacture. Farmers producing so much, factories so much, exchange being carried on in such a way, they analyze the sale, the profit the net gain or the surplus value,the wages, the taxes, banking, and so on.

But after having followed them so far, we are none the wiser, and if we ask them: "How is it that millions of human beings are in want of bread, when every family could grow sufficient wheat to feed ten, twenty, and even a hundred people annually?" they answer us by droning the same anthem- division of labour, wages, surplus value, capital, etc.- arriving at the same conclusion, that production is insufficient to satisfy all needs; a conclusion which, if true, does not answer the question: "Can or cannot man by his labour produce the bread he needs? And if he cannot, what is hindering him?"

Here are 350 million Europeans. They need so much bread, so much meat, wine, milk, eggs, and butter every year. They need so many houses, so much clothing. This is the minimum of their needs. Can they produce all this? and if they can, will there then be left sufficient leisure for art,science, and amusement?- in a word, for everything that is not comprised in the category of absolute necessities? If the answer is in the affirmative, -What hinders them going ahead? What must they do to remove obstacles? Is time needed? Let them take it! But let us not lose sight of the aim of production- the satisfaction of needs.

If the most imperious needs of man remain unsatisfied, what must he do to increase the productivity of his work? And is there no other cause? Might it not be that production, having lost sight of the *needs* of man, has strayed in an absolutely wrong direction, and that its organization is at fault? And as we can prove that such is the case, let us see how to reorganize production so as to really satisfy all needs.

This seems to us the only right way of facing things. The only way that would allow of Political Economy becoming a science- the Science of Social Physiology.

It is evident that when this science will treat of production, as it is at present carried on by civilized nations, by Hindoo communes, or by savages, it will hardly state facts otherwise than the economists state them now; that is to say as a simple descriptive chapter, analogous to *descriptive* chapters of Zoology and Botany. But if this chapter were written to throw light on the economy of energy, necessary to satisfy human needs, the chapter would gain in precision, as well as in descriptive value. It would clearly prove the frightful waste of human energy under the present system, and would admit, as we do, that as long as this system exists,the needs of humanity will never be satisfied.

The point of view, we see, would be entirely changed. Behind the loom that weaves so many yards of cloth, behind the steel-plate perforator, and behind the safe in which dividends are hoarded, we should see man, the artisan of production, more often than not excluded from the feast he has prepared for others. We should also understand that the standpoint being wrong, so-called laws of value and exchange are but a very false explanation of events, as they happen nowadays; and that things will come to pass very differently when production is organized in such a manner as to meet all needs of society.

II

There is not one single principle of Political Economy that does not change its aspect if you look at it from our point of view.

Take, for instance, over-production, a word which every day re-echoes in our ears. Is there a single economist, academician, or candidate for academical honours, who has not supported arguments, proving that economic crises are due to overproduction- that at a given moment more cotton, more cloth, more watches are produced than are needed! Have not men accused of "rapacity" the capitalists who are obstinately bent on producing more than can possibly be consumed! But on careful examination all these reasonings prove unsound. In fact, Is there a commodity among those in universal use which is produced in greater quantity than need be? Examine one by one all commodities sent out by countries exporting on a large scale,and you will see that nearly all are produced in *insufficient* quantities for the inhabitants of the countries exporting them.

It is not a surplus of wheat that the Russian peasant sends to Europe. The most plentiful harvests of wheat and rye in. European Russia only yieldenough for the population. And as a rule the peasant deprives himself of what he actually needs when he sells his wheat or rye to pay rent and taxes.

It is not a surplus of coal that England sends to the four corners of the globe, because only three-quarters of a ton, per head of population, annually, remain for home domestic consumption, and millions of Englishmen are deprived of fire in the winter, or have only just enough to boil a few vegetables. In fact, setting aside useless luxuries, there is in England, which exports more than any other country, but a single commodity in universal use- cottons- whose production is sufficiently great to exceed the needs of the community. Yet when we look upon the rags that pass for wearing apparel worn by over a third of the inhabitants of the United Kingdom, we are led to ask ourselves whether the cottons exported would not, within a trifle, suit the *real* needs of the population?

As a rule it is not a surplus that is exported, though it may have been so originally. The fable of the barefooted shoemaker is as true of nations as it was formerly of artisans. We export the necessary commodities. And we do so, because the workmen cannot buy with their wages what they have produced, and pay besides the rent and interest to the capitalist and the banker.

Not only does the ever-growing need of comfort remain unsatisfied, but strict necessaries are often wanting. "Surplus production" does, therefore, not exist, at least not in the sense which is given to it by the theorists of Political Economy.

Taking another point- all economists tell us that there is a well-proved law: "Man produces more than he consumes." After he has lived on the proceeds of his toil, there remains a surplus. Thus, a family of cultivators produces enough to feed several families, and so forth.

For us, this oft-repeated sentence has no sense. If it meant that each generation leaves something to future generations, it would be true; thus, for example, a farmer plants a tree that will live, maybe, for thirty, forty, or a hundred years, and whose fruits will still be gathered by the farmer's grandchildren. Or he clears a few acres of virgin soil, and we say that the heritage of future generations has been increased by that much. Roads, bridges, canals, his house and his furniture are so much wealth bequeathed to succeeding generations.

But this is not what is meant. We are told that the cultivator produces more than he need consume. Rather should they say that, the State having always taken from him a large share of his produce for taxes, the priest for tithe, and the landlord for rent, a whole class of men has been created, who formerly consumed what they produced- save what was set aside for unforeseen accidents, or expenses incurred in afforestation, roads, etc.- but who to-day are compelled to live very poorly, from hand to mouth, the remainder having been taken from them by the State, the landlord, the priest, and the usurer.

Let us also observe that if the needs of the individual are our starting-point, we cannot fail to reach Communism, an organization which enables us to satisfy all needs in the most thorough and economical way. While if we start from our present method of production, and aim at gain and surplus value, without taking into account if production corresponds to the satisfaction of needs, we necessarily arrive at Capitalism, or at most at Collectivism- both being but divers forms of our wages' system.

In fact, when we consider the needs of the individual and of society, and the means which man has resorted to in order to satisfy them during his varied phases of development, we are convinced of the necessity of systematizing our efforts, instead of producing haphazard as we do nowadays. It grows evident that the appropriation by a few of all riches not consumed,and transmitted from one generation to another, is not in the general interest.We can state as a fact that owing to these methods the needs of three-quarters of society are not satisfied, and that the present waste of human strength is the more useless and the more criminal.

We discover, moreover, that the most advantageous use of all commodities would be, for each of them, to go, first, for satisfying those needs which are the most pressing: that, in other words, the so-called "value in use" of a commodity does not depend on a simple whim, as has often been affirmed, but on the satisfaction it brings to real needs.

Communism- that is to say, an organization which would correspond to a view of Consumption, Production, and Exchange, taken as; a whole — therefore becomes the logical consequence of the comprehension of things, the only one, in our opinion,that is really scientific.

A society that will satisfy the needs of all, and which will know how to organize production, will also have to make a clean sweep of several prejudices concerning industry, and first of all of the theory often preached by economists- *The Division of Labour* theory- which we are going to discuss in the next chapter.

CHAPTER-XV

THE DIVISION OF LABOUR

I

Political Economy has always confined itself to stating facts occurring in society, and justifying them in the interest of the dominant class. Thus it is in favour of the division of labour created by industry. Having found it profitable to capitalists it has set it up as a principle.

Look at the village smith, said Adam Smith, the father of modern Political Economy. If he has never been accustomed to making nails he will only succeed by hard toil in forging two to three hundred a day, and even then they will be bad. But if this same smith has never done anything but nails, he will easily supply as many as two thousand three hundred in the course of a day. And Smith hastened to the conclusion—"Divide labour, specialize, go on specializing; let us have smiths who only know how to make heads or points of nails, and by this means we shall produce more. We shall grow rich."

That a smith sentenced for life to the making of heads of nails would lose all interest in his work, would be entirely at the mercy of his employer with his limited handicraft, would be out of work four months out of twelve, and that his wages would decrease when he could be easily replaced by an apprentice, Smith did not think of it when he exclaimed—"Long live the division of labour. This is the real gold-mine that will enrich the nation!" And all joined in the cry.

And later on, when a Sismondi or a J. B. Say began to understand that the division of labour, instead of enriching the whole nation, only enriches the rich, and that the worker, who for life is doomed to making the eighteenth part of a pin, grows stupid and sinks into poverty—what did official economists propose? Nothing! They did not say to themselves that by a lifelong grind at one and the same mechanical toil the worker would lose his intelligence and his spirit of invention, and that, on the contrary, a variety of occupations would result in considerably augmenting the productivity of a nation. But this is the very issue now before us.

If, however, only economists preached the permanent and often hereditary division of labour, we might allow them to preach it as much as they pleased. But ideas taught by doctors of science filter into men's minds and pervert them; and from repeatedly hearing the division of labour, profits, interest, credit, etc., spoken of as problems long since solved, men, and workers too, end by arguing like economists, and by venerating the same fetishes.

Thus we see a number of socialists, even those who have not feared to point out the mistakes of science, justifying the division of labour. Talk to them about the organization of work during the Revolution, and they answer that the division of labour must be maintained; that if you sharpened pins before the Revolution you must go on sharpening them after. True, you will not have to work more than five hours a day, but you will have to sharpen pins all your life, while others will make designs for machines that will enable you to sharpen hundreds of millions of pins during your lifetime; and others again will be specialists in the higher branches of literature, science, and art, etc. You were born to sharpen pins while Pasteur was born to invent the inoculation against anthrax, and the Revolution will leave you both to your respective employments. Well, it is this horrible principle, so noxious to society, so brutalizing to the individual, source of so much harm, that we propose to discuss in its divers manifestations.

We know the consequences of the division of labour full well. It is evident that we are divided into two classes: on the one hand, producers who consume very little and are exempt from thinking because they only do physical work, and who work badly because their brains remain inactive; and on the other hand, the consumers, who, producing little or hardly anything, have the privilege of thinking for the others, and who think badly because the whole world of those who toil with their hands is unknown to them. The labourers of the soil know nothing of machinery those who work at machinery ignore everything about agriculture. The ideal of modern industry is a child *tending* a machine that he cannot and must not understand, and a foreman who fines him if his attention flags for a moment. The ideal of industrial agriculture is to do away with the agricultural labourer altogether and to set a man who does odd jobs to tend a steam-plough or a threshing-machine. The division of labour means labelling and stamping men for life—some to splice ropes in factories, some to be foremen in a business, others to shove huge coal-baskets in a particular part of a mine; but none of them to have any idea of machinery as a whole, nor of business, nor of mines. And thereby they destroy the love of work and the capacity for invention that, at the beginning of modern industry, created the machinery on which we pride ourselves so much.

What they have done for individuals, they also wanted to do for nations. Humanity was to be divided into national workshops, having each its speciality. Russia, we were taught, was destined by nature to grow corn; England to spin cotton; Belgium to weave cloth; while Switzerland was to train nurses and governesses. Moreover, each separate city was to establish a speciality. Lyons was to weave silk, Auvergne to make lace, and Paris fancy articles. Economists believed that specialization opened an immense field for production and consumption, and that an era of limitless wealth for mankind was at hand.

But these great hopes vanished as fast as technical knowledge spread abroad. As long as England stood alone as a weaver of cotton, and as a metal-worker on a large scale; as long as only Paris made artistic fancy articles, etc., all went well, economists could preach so-called division of labour without being refuted.

But a new current of thought induced all civilized nations to manufacture for themselves. They found it advantageous to produce what they formerly received from other countries, or from their colonies, which in their turn aimed at emancipating themselves from the mother-country. Scientific discoveries universalized the methods of production and henceforth it was useless to pay an exorbitant price abroad for what could easily be produced at home. Does not then this industrial revolution strike a crushing blow at the theory of the division of labour which was supposed to be so sound?

CHAPTER-XVI

THE DECENTRALIZATION OF INDUSTRY

I

After the Napoleonic wars Britain all but succeeded in ruining the main industries which had sprung up in France at the end of the preceding century. She became also mistress of the seas and had no rivals of importance. She took in the situation, and knew how to turn its privileges and advantages to account. She established an industrial monopoly, and, imposing upon her neighbours her prices for the goods she alone could manufacture, accumulated riches upon riches.

But as the middle-class Revolution of the eighteenth century abolished serfdom and created a proletariat in France, industry, hampered for a time in its flight, soared again, and from the second half of the nineteenth century France ceased to be a tributary of England for manufactured goods. To-day she too has grown into a nation with an export trade. She sells far more than sixty million pounds' worth of manufactured goods, and two-thirds of these goods are fabrics. The number of Frenchmen working for export or living by their foreign trade, is estimated at three millions.

France is therefore no longer England's tributary. In her turn she has striven to monopolize certain branches of foreign industry, such as silks and ready-made clothes, and has reaped immense profits therefrom; but she is on the point of losing this monopoly for ever, as England is on the point of losing the monopoly of cotton goods.

Travelling eastwards, industry has reached Germany. Fifty years ago Germany was a tributary of England and France for most manufactured commodities in the higher branches of industry. It is no longer so. In the course of the last forty-five years, and especially since the Franco-German war, Germany has completely reorganized her industry. The new factories are stocked with the best machinery; the latest creations of industrial art in cotton goods from Manchester, or in silks from Lyons, etc., are now realized in recent German factories. It took two or three generations of workers, at Lyons and Manchester, to construct the modern machinery; but Germany adopted it in its perfected state. Technical schools, adapted to the needs of industry, supply the factories with an army of intelligent workmen—practical engineers, who can work with hand and brain. German industry starts at the point which was only reached by Manchester and Lyons after fifty years of groping in the dark, of exertion and experiments.

It follows that as Germany manufactures as well at home, she diminishes her imports from France and England year by year. She has not only become their rival in manufactured goods in Asia and in Africa, but also in London and in Paris. Shortsighted people may cry out against the Frankfort Treaty, they may explain German competition by little differences in railway tariffs; they may linger on the petty side of questions and neglect great historical facts. But it is none the less certain that the main industries, formerly in the hands of England and France, have progressed eastward, and in Germany they found a country, young, full of energy, possessing an intelligent middle class, and eager in its turn to enrich itself by foreign trade.

While Germany freed itself from subjection to France and England, manufactured her own cotton cloth, constructed her own machines—in fact, manufactured all commodities—the main industries took also root in Russia, where the development of manufacture is the more surprising as it sprang up but yesterday.

At the time of the abolition of serfdom in 1861, Russia hardly had any factories. Everything they needed—machines, rails, railway-engines, rich materials—came from the West. Twenty years later she possessed already 85,000 factories, and the goods from these factories had increased fourfold in value.

The old machinery was superseded, and now nearly all the steel in use in Russia, three-quarters of the iron, two-thirds of the coal, all railway engines, railway-carriages, rails, nearly all steamers, are made in Russia.

Russia, destined—so wrote economists—to remain an agricultural territory, has rapidly developed into a manufacturing country. She orders hardly anything from England, and very little from Germany.

Economists hold the customs responsible for these facts, and yet cottons manufactured in Russia are sold at the same price as in London. Capital taking no cognizance of fatherland, German and English capitalists, accompanied by engineers and foremen of their own nationalities, have introduced in Russia and in Poland manufactories, the excellence of whose goods compete with the best from England. If customs were abolished to-morrow, manufacture would only gain by it. Not long ago the British manufacturers delivered another hard blow to the imports of cloth and woollens from the West. They set up in southern and middle Russia immense wool factories, stocked with the most perfect machinery from Bradford, and already now Russia hardly imports more than a few pieces of English cloth and French woollen fabrics as samples.

The main industries not only move eastward, they are spreading to the southern peninsulas. The Turin Exhibition of 1884 has already shown the progress made in Italian manufactured produce, and, let us not make any mistake about it, the mutual hatred of the French and Italian middle classes has no other origin than their industrial rivalry. Spain is also becoming an industrial country; while in the East, Bohemia has suddenly sprung up to importance as a new centre of manufactures, provided with perfected machinery and applying the best scientific methods.

We might also mention Hungary's rapid progress in the main industries, but let us rather take Brazil as an example. Economists sentenced Brazil to cultivate cotton for ever, to export it in its raw state, and to receive cotton-cloth from Europe in exchange. In fact, forty years ago Brazil had only nine wretched little cotton factories with 385 spindles. To-day there are 108 cotton-mills, possessing 715,000 spindles and 26,050 looms, which tllrow 234 million yards of textiles on the market annually.

Even Mexico is setting about manufacturing cotton-cloth, instead of importing it from Europe. As to the United States they have quite freed themselves from European tutelage, and have triumphally developed their manufacturing powers.

But it was India which gave the most striking proof against the specialization of national industry.

We all know the theory: the great European nations need colonies, for colonies send raw material—cotton fibre, unwashed wool, spices, etc., to the mother-land. And the mother-land, under pretence of sending them manufactured wares, gets rid of her burnt stuffs, her machine scrap-iron and every thing which she no longer has use for. It costs her little or nothing, and none the less the articles are sold at exorbitant prices.

Such was the theory—such was the practice for a long time. In London and Manchester fortunes were made while India was being ruined. In the India Museum in London unheard-of riches, collected in Calcutta and Bombay by English merchants, are to be seen.

But other English merchants and capitalists conceived the very simple idea that it would be more expedient to exploit the natives of India by making cotton-cloth in India itself, than to import from twenty to twenty-four million pounds' worth of goods annually.

At first a series of experiments ended in failure. Indian weavers—artists and experts in their own craft—could not inure themselves to factory life; the machinery sent from Liverpool was bad; the climate had to be taken into account; and merchants had to adapt themselves to new conditions, now fully observed, before British India could become the menacing rival of the Mother-land she is to-day.

She now possesses 200 cotton factories which employ about 196,400 workmen, and contain 5,231,OOO spindles and 48,400 looms, and 38 jute mills, with 409,000 spindles. She exports annually to China, to the Dutch Indies, and to Africa, nearly eight million pounds' worth of the same white cotton-cloth, said to be England's speciality. And while English workmen are unemployed and in great want, Indian women weave cotton by machinery for the Far East at the rate of sixpence a day. In short, intelligent manufacturers are fully aware that the day is not far off when they will not know what to do with the "factory hands" who formerly weaved cotton-cloth exported from England. Besides which it is becoming more and more evident that India will not import a single ton of iron from England. The initial difficulties in using the coal and the iron ore obtained in India have been overcome; and foundries, rivalling those in England, have been built on the shores of the Indian Ocean.

Colonies competing with the mother-land in its production of manufactured goods, such is the factor which will regulate economy in the twentieth century.

And why should India not manufacture ? What should be the hindrance ? Capital?—But capital goes wherever there are men, poor enough to be exploited. Knowledge?—But knowledge recognizes no national barriers. Technical skill of the worker?—No. Are, then, Hindoo workmen inferior to the 237,000 boys and girls, not eighteen years old, at present working in the English textile factories?

II

After having glanced at national industries it would be very interesting to turn to special industries.

Let us take silk, for example, an eminently French product in the first half of the nineteenth century. We all know how Lyons became the emporium of the silk trade. At first raw silk was gathered in southern France, till little by little they ordered it from Italy, from Spain, from Austria, from the Caucasus, and from Japan, for the manufacture of their silk fabrics. In 1875, out of five million kilos of raw silk converted into stuffs in the vicinity of Lyons, there were only four hundred thousand kilos of French silk. But if Lyons manufactured imported silk, why should not Switzerland, Germany, Russia, do as much? Silk weaving developed indeed in the villages round Zurich. BÃ¢le became a great centre of the silk trade. The Caucasian Administration engaged women from Marseilles and workmen from Lyons to teach Georgians the perfected rearing of silkworms, and the art of converting silk into fabrics to the Caucasian peasants. Austria followed. Then Germany, with the help of Lyons workmen, built great silk factories. The United States did likewise in Paterson.

And to-day the silk trade is no longer a French monopoly. Silks are made in Germany, in Austria, in the United States, and in England. In winter, Caucasian peasants weave silk handkerchiefs at a wage that would mean starvation to the silkweavers of Lyons. Italy sends silks to France; and Lyons, which in 1870-4 exported 460 million francs' worth of silk fabrics, exports now only one-half of that amount. In fact, the time is not far off when Lyons will only send higher class goods and a few novelties as patterns to Germany, Russia, and Japan.

And so it is in all industries. Belgium has no longer the cloth monopoly; cloth is made in Germany, in Russia, in Austria, in the United States. Switzerland and the French Jura have no longer a clockwork monopoly: watches are made every where. Scotland no longer refines sugar for Russia: Russian sugar is imported into England. Italy, although neither possessing coal nor iron, makes its own ironclads and engines for her steamers. Chemical industry is no longer an English monopoly; sulphuric acid and soda are made even in the Urals. Steam-engines, made at Winterthur, have acquired everywhere a wide reputation, and at the present moment, Switzerland, that has neither coal nor iron—nothing but excellent technical schools—makes machinery better and cheaper than England. So ends the theory of Exchange.

The tendency of trade, as for all else, is toward decentralization.

Every nation finds it advantageous to combine agriculture with the greatest possible variety of foundries and manufactories. The specialization, of which economists spoke so highly, enriched a number of capitalists but is now of no use. On the contrary, it is to the advantage of every region, every nation, to grow their own wheat, their own vegetables, and to manufacture all produce they consume at home. This diversity is the surest pledge of the complete development of production by mutual co-operation, and the moving cause of progress, while specialization is a hindrance to progress.

Agriculture can only prosper in proximity to factories. And no sooner does a single factory appear than an infinite variety of other factories must spring up around, so that, mutually supporting and stimulating one another by their inventions, they increase their productivity.

III

It is foolish indeed to export wheat and import flour, to export wool and import cloth, to export iron and import machinery; not only because transportation is a waste of time and money, but, above all, because a country with no developed industry inevitably remains behind the times in agriculture; because a country with no large factories to bring steel to a finished condition is also backward in all other industries; and lastly, because the industrial and technical capacities of the nation remain undeveloped.

In the world of production everything holds together nowadays. Cultivation of the soil is no longer possible without machinery, without great irrigation works, without railways, without manure factories. And to adapt this machinery, these railways, these irrigation engines, etc., to local conditions, a certain spirit of invention, a certain amount of technical skill, that lie dormant as long as spades and ploughshares are the only implements of cultivation, must be developed.

If fields are to be properly cultivated, and are to yield the abundant harvests man has the right to expect, it is essential that workshops, foundries, and factories develop within the reach of the fields. A variety of occupations, a variety of skill arising therefrom end working together for a common aim—these are the genuine forces of progress.

And now let us imagine the inhabitants of a city or a territory—whether vast or small—stepping for the first time on to the path of the Social Revolution.

We are sometimes told that "nothing will have changed": that the mines, the factories, etc., will be expropriated, and proclaimed national or communal property, that every man will go back to his usual work, and that the Revolution will then be accomplished.

But this is a dream: the Social Revolution cannot take place so simply.

We have already mentioned that should the Revolution break out to-morrow in Paris, Lyons, or any other city—should the workers lay hands on factories, houses, and banks, present production would be completely revolutionized by this simple fact.

International commerce will come to a standstill; so also will the importation of foreign bread-stuffs; the circulation of commodities and of provisions will be paralyzed. And then, the city or territory in revolt will be compelled to provide for itself, and to reorganize production. If it fails to do so, it is death. If it succeeds, it will revolutionize the economic life of the country.

The quantity of imported provisions having decreased, consumption having increased, one million Parisians working for exportation purposes having been thrown out of work, a great number of things imported to-day from distant or neighbouring countries not reaching their destination, fancy-trade being temporarily at a standstill, What will the inhabitants have to eat six months after the Revolution?

We think that when the stores are empty, the masses will seek to obtain their food from the land. They will be compelled to cultivate the soil, to combine agricultural production with industrial production in Paris and its environs. They will have to abandon the merely ornamental trades and consider the most urgent need—bread.

Citizens will be obliged to become agriculturists. Not in the same manner as peasants who wear themselves out, ploughing for a wage that barely provides them with sufficient food for the year' but by following the principles of market-gardeners' intensive agriculture, applied on a large scale by means of the best machinery that man has invented or can invent. They will till the land—not, how ever, like the country beast of burden a Paris jeweller would object to that. They will reorganize cultivation, not in ten years' time, but at once, during the revolutionary struggles, from fear of being worsted by the enemy.

Agriculture will have to be carried on by intelligent beings; availing themselves of their knowledge, organizing themselves in joyous gangs for pleasant work, like the men who, a hundred years ago, worked in the Champ de Mars for the Feast of the Federation—a work of delight, when not carried to excess, when scientifically organized, when man invents and improves his tools and is conscious of being a useful member of the community.

Of course, they will not only cultivate, they will also produce those things which they formerly used to order from foreign parts. And let us not forget that for the inhabitants of a revolted territory, "foreign parts" may include all districts that have not joined in the revolutionary movement. During the Revolutions of 1793 and 1871 Paris was made to feel that "foreign parts" meant even the country district at her very gates. The speculator in grains at Troyes starved the sansculottes of Paris more effectually than the German armies brought on French soil by the Versailles conspirators. The revolted city will be compelled to do without "foreigners," and why not? France invented beetroot sugar when sugar-cane ran short during the continental blockade. Parisians discovered salt petre in their cellars when they no longer received any from abroad. Shall we be inferior to our grandfathers, who with difficulty lisped the first words of science?

A revolution is more than the destruction of a political system. It implies the awakening of human intelligence, the increasing of the inventive spirit tenfold, a hundredfold; it is the dawn of a new, science—the science of men like Laplace, Lamarck, Lavoisier. It is a revolution in the minds of men, more than in their institutions.

And economists tell us to return to our workshops, as if passing through a revolution were going home after a walk in the Epping forest!

To begin with, the sole fact of having laid hands on middle-class property implies the necessity of completely reorganizing the whole of economic life in workshops, in dockyards, and in factories.

And the revolution will not fail to act in this direction. Should Paris, during the social revolution, be cut off from the world for a year or two by the supporters of middle-class rule, its millions of intellects, not yet depressed by factory life—that City of little trades which stimulate the spirit of invention—will show the world what man's brain can accomplish without asking any help from without, but the motor force of the sun that gives light, the power of the wind that sweeps away impurities, and the silent life-forces at work in the earth we tread on.

We shall see then what a variety of trades, mutually co-operating on a spot of the globe and animated by the social revolution, can do to feed, clothe, house, and supply with all manner of luxuries millions of intelligent men.

We need write no fiction to prove this. What we are sure of, what has already been experimented upon, and recognized as practical, would suffice to carry it into effect, if the attempt were fertilized, vivified by the daring inspiration of the Revolution and the spontaneous impulse of the masses.

CHAPTER-XVII

AGRICULTURE

I

Political Economy has often been reproached with drawing all its deductions from the decidedly false principle, that the only incentive capable of forcing a man to augment his power of production is personal interest in its narrowest sense.

The reproach is perfectly true; so true that epochs of great industrial discoveries and true progress in industry are precisely those in which the happiness of all was the aim pursued, and in which personal enrichment was least thought of. Great investigators and great inventors aimed, without doubt, at the emancipation of mankind. And if Watt, Stephenson, Jacquard, etc., could have only foreseen what a state of misery their sleepless nights would bring to the workers, they would probably have burned their designs and broken their models.

Another principle that pervades Political Economy is just as false. It is the tacit admission, common to all economists, that if there is often over-production in certain branches, a society will nevertheless never have sufficient products to satisfy the wants of all, and that consequently the day will never come when nobody will be forced to sell his labour in exchange for wages. This tacit admission is found at the basis of all theories and the so-called "laws" taught by economists.

And yet it is certain that the day when any civilized association of individuals would ask itself, what are the needs of all, and the means of satisfying them, it would see that, in industry as in agriculture, it already possesses sufficient to provide abundantly for all needs, on condition that it knows how to apply these means to satisfy real needs.

That this is true as regards industry no one can contest. Indeed, it suffices to study the processes already in use to extract coals and ore, to obtain steel and work it, to manufacture what is used for clothing, etc., in large industrial establishments, in order to perceive that we could already increase our production fourfold and yet economize work.

We go further. We assert that agriculture is in the same position: the labourer, like the manufacturer, already possesses the means to increase his production, not only fourfold but tenfold, and he will be able to put it into practice as soon as he feels the need of it, as soon as the socialist organization of work will be established instead of the present capitalistic one.

Each time agriculture is spoken of, men imagine a peasant bending over the plough, throwing badly sorted corn haphazard into the ground and waiting anxiously for what the good or bad season will bring forth; or a family working from morn to night and reaping as reward a rude bed, dry bread, and coarse beverage. In a word, they picture "the wild beast" of La Bruyere.

And for this man, thus subjected to misery, the utmost relief society proposes is to reduce his taxes or his rent. But they do not even dare to imagine a cultivator standing erect, taking leisure, and producing by a few hours' work per day sufficient food to nourish, not only his own family, but a hundred men more at the least. In their most glowing dreams of thc future Socialists do not go beyond American extensive culture, which, after all, is but the infancy of agricultural art.

The agriculturist has broader ideas to-day—his conceptions are on a far grander scale. He only asks for a fraction of an acre in order to produce sufficient vegetables for a family; and to feed twenty-five horned beasts he needs no more space than he formerly required to feed one; his aim is to make his own soil, to defy seasons and climate, to warm both air and earth around the young plant; to produce, in a word, on one acre what he used to crop on fifty acres, and that without any excessive fatigue—by greatly reducing, on the contrary, the total of former labour. He knows that we will be able to feed everybody by giving to the culture of the fields no more time than what each can give with pleasure and joy.

This is the present tendency of agriculture.

While scientific men, led by Liebig, the creator of the chemical theory of agriculture, often got on the wrong tack in their love of mere theories, unlettered agriculturists opened up new roads to prosperity. Market-gardeners of Paris, Troyes, Rouen, Scotch and English gardeners, Flemish farmers, peasants of Jersey, Guernsey, and farmers on the Scilly Isles have opened up such large horizons that the mind hesitates to grasp them. While up till lately a family of peasants needed at least seventeen to twenty acres to live on the produce of the soil—and we know how peasants live—we can no longer say what is the minimum area on which all that is necessary to a family can be grown, even including articles of luxury, if the soil is worked by means of intensive culture.

Ten years ago it could already be asserted that a population of thirty million individuals could live very well, without importing anything, on what could be grown in Great Britain. But now, when we see the progress recently made in France as well as in England, and when we contemplate the new horizons which open before us, we can say that in cultivating the earth as it is already cultivated in many places, even on poor soils, fifty or sixty million inhabitants to the territory of Great Britain would still be a very feeble proportion to what man could exact from the soil.

In any case (as we are about to demonstrate) we may consider it as absolutely proved that if to-morrow Paris and the two departments of Seine and of Seine-et-Oise organized themselves as an Anarchist commune, in which all worked with their hands, and if the entire universe refused to send them a single bushel of wheat, a single head of cattle, a single basket of fruit, and left them only the territory of the two departments, they could not only produce corn, meat, and vegetables necessary for themselves, but also articles of luxury in sufficient quantities for all.

And, in addition, we affirm that the sum total of this labour would be far less than that expended at present to feed these people with corn harvested in Auvergne and Russia, with vegetables produced a little everywhere by extensive agriculture, and with fruit grown in the South.

It is self-evident that we in nowise desire "all" exchange to be suppressed, nor that each region should strive to produce that which will only grow in its climate by a more or less artificial culture. But we care to draw attention to the fact that the theory of exchange, such as is understood to-day, is strangely exaggerated—that exchange is often useless and even harmful. We assert, moreover, that people have never had a right conception of the immense labour of Southern wine growers, nor of that of Russian and Hungarian corn growers, whose excessive labour could also be very much reduced if they adopted intensive culture, instead of their present system of extensive agriculture.

II

It would be impossible to quote here the mass of facts on which we base our assertions. We are therefore obliged to refer our readers who want further information to another book, "Fields, Factories, and Workshops." Above all we earnestly invite those who are interested in the question to read several excellent works published in France and elsewhere, and of which we give a list at the close of this book (1). As to the inhabitants of large towns, who have as yet no real notion of what agriculture can be, we advise them to explore the surrounding market- gardens and study the cultivation. They need but observe and question market-gardeners, and a new world will be open to them. They will thus be able to see what European agriculture may be in the twentieth century; and they will understand with what force the social revolution will be armed when we know the secret of taking everything we need from the soil.

A few facts will suffice to show that our assertions are in no way exaggerated. We only wish them to be preceded by a few general remarks.

We know in what a wretched condition European agriculture is. If the cultivator of the soil is not plundered by the landowner, he is robbed by the State. If the State taxes him moderately, the money-lender enslaves him by means of promissory notes, and soon turns him into the simple tenant of a soil belonging in reality to a financial company. The landlord, the State, and the banker thus plunder the cultivator by means of rent, taxes, and interest. The sum varies in each country, but it never falls below the quarter, very often the half of the raw produce. In France agriculturists paid the State quite recently as much as 44 per cent of the gross produce.

Moreover, the share of the owner and the State always goes on increasing. As soon as the cultivator has obtained more plentiful crops by prodigies of labour, invention, or initiative, the tribute he will owe to the landowner, the State, and the banker will augment in proportion. If he doubles the number of bushels reaped per acre, rent will be doubled and taxes too, and the State will take care to raise them still more if the prices go up. And so on. In short, everywhere the cultivator of the soil works twelve to sixteen hours a day; these three vultures take from him everything he might lay by; they rob him everywhere of what would enable him to improve his culture. This is why agriculture progresses so slowly.

The cultivator can only occasionally make some progress, in some exceptional regions, under quite exceptional circumstances, following upon a quarrel between the three vampires. And yet we have said nothing about the tribute every cultivator pays to the manufacturer. Every machine, every spade, every barrel of chemical manure, is sold to him at three or four times its real cost. Nor let us forget the middleman, who levies the lion's share of the earth's produce.

This is why, during all this century of invention and progress, agriculture has only improved from time to time on very limited areas.

Happily there have always been small oases, neglected for some time by the vultures; and here we learn what intensive agriculture can produce for mankind. Let us mention a few examples.

In the American prairies (which, however, only yield meagre spring wheat crops, from 7 to 15 bushels an acre, and even these are often marred by periodical droughts), 500 men, working only during eight months, produce the annual food of 50,000 people. With all the improvements of the last few years, one man's yearly labour (300 days) yields, delivered in Chicago as flour, the yearly food of 250 men. Here the result is obtained by a great economy in manual labour: on those vast plains, which the eye cannot encompass, ploughing, harvesting, thrashing, are organized in almost military fashion. There is no useless running to and fro, no loss of time—all is done with parade-like precision.

This is agriculture on a large scale—extensive agriculture, which takes the soil from nature without seeking to improve it. When the earth has yielded ail it can, they leave it; they seek elsewhere for a virgin soil, to be exhausted in its turn. But there is also "intensive" agriculture, which is already worked, and will be more and more so, by machinery. Its object is to cultivate a limited space well, to manure, to improve, to concentrate work, and to obtain the largest crop possible. This kind of culture spreads every year, and whereas agriculturists in the south of France and on the fertile plains of Western America are content with an average crop of 11 to 15 bushels per acre by extensive culture, they reap regularly 39 even 55, and sometimes 60 bushels per acre in the north of France. The annual consumption of a man is thus obtained from less than a quarter of an acre.

And the more intense the culture is, the less work is expended to obtain a bushel of wheat. Machinery replaces man at the preliminary work and for the improvements needed by the land—such as draining, clearing of stones—which will double the crops in future, once and for ever. Sometimes nothing but keeping the soil free of weeds without manuring, allows an average soil to yield excellent crops from year to year. It has been done for twenty years in succession at Rothamstead, in Hertfordshire.

Let us not write an agricultural romance, but be satisfied with a crop of 44 bushels per acre. That needs no exceptional soil, but merely a rational culture; and let us see what it means.

The 3,600,000 individuals who inhabit the two departments of Seine and Seine-et-Oise consume yearly for their food a little less than 22 million bushels of cereals, chiefly wheat; and in our hypothesis they would have to cultivate, in order to obtain this crop, 494,200 acres out of the 1,507,300 acres which they possess. It is evident they would not cultivate them with spades. That would need too much time—96 work-days of 5 hours per acre. It would be preferable to improve the soil once for all—to drain what needed to be drained to level what needed levelling, to clear the soil of stones, were it even necessary to spend 5 million days of 5 hours in this preparatory work—an average of 10 work-days to each acre.

Then they would plough with the steam-digger, which would take one and three-fifths of a day per acre, and they would give another one and three-fifths of a day for working with the double plough. Seeds would be sorted by steam instead of taken haphazard, and they would be carefully sown in rows instead of being thrown to the four winds. Now all this work would not take

10 days of 5 hours per acre if the work were done under good conditions. But if 10 million work-days are given to good culture during 3 or 4 years, the result will be later on crops of 44 to 55 bushels per acre by only working half the time.

Fifteen million work-days will have thus been spent to give bread to a population of 3,600,000 inhabitants. And the work would be such that each could do it without having muscles of steel, or without having even worked the ground before. The initiative and the general distribution of work would come from those who know the soil. As to the work itself, there is no townsman of either sex so enfeebled as to be incapable of looking after machines and of contributing his share to agrarian work after a few hours' apprenticeship.

Well, when we consider that in the present chaos there are, in a city like Paris, without counting the unemployed of the upper classes, about 100,000 men out of work in their several trades, we see that the power lost in our present organization would alone suffice to give, with a rational culture, bread necessary to the three or four million inhabitants of the two departments.

We repeat, this is no fancy dream, and we have not spoken of the truly intensive agriculture. We have not depended upon the wheat (obtained in three years by Mr. Hallett) of which one grain, replanted, produced 5000 or 6000, and occasionally 10,000 grains, which would give the wheat necessary for a family of five individuals on an area of 120 square yards. On the contrary, we have only mentioned what has been already achieved by numerous farmers in France, England, Belgium, etc., and what might be done to-morrow with the experience and knowledge acquired already by practice on a large scale.

But without a revolution, neither to-morrow, nor after to-morrow will see it done, because it is not to the interest of landowners and capitalists; and because peasants who would find their profit in it have neither the knowledge nor the money, nor the time to obtain what is necessary to go ahead.

The present society has not yet reached this stage. But let Parisians proclaim an Anarchist Commune, and they will of necessity come to it, because they will not be foolish enough to continue making luxurious toys (which Vienna, Warsaw, and Berlin make as well already) and to run the risk of being left without bread.

Moreover, agricultural work, by the help of machinery, would soon become the most attractive and the most joyful of all occupations.

"We have had enough jewellery and enough dolls' clothes," they would say; "it is high time for the workers to recruit their strength in agriculture, to go in search of vigour, of impressions of nature, of the joy of life, that they have forgotten in the dark factories of the suburbs."

In the Middle Ages it was Alpine pasture lands, rather than guns, which allowed the Swiss to shake off lords and kings. Modern agriculture will allow a city in revolt to free itself from the combined bourgeois forces.

III

We have seen how the 3½ million inhabitants of the two departments round Paris could find ample bread by cultivating only a third of their territory. Let us now pass on to cattle.

Englishmen, who eat much meat, consume on an average a little less than 220 lb. a year per adult. Supposing all meats consumed were oxen, that makes a little less than the third of an ox. An ox a year for 5 individuals (including children) is already a sufficient ration. For 3½ million inhabitants this would make an annual consumption of 700,000 head of cattle.

To-day, with the pasture system, we need at least 5 million acres to nourish 660,000 head of cattle. This makes 9 acres per each head of horned cattle. Nevertheless, with prairies moderately watered by spring water (as recently done on thousands of acres in the south-west of France), 1¼ million acres already suffice. But if intensive culture is practiced, and beetroot is grown for fodder, you only need a quarter of that area, that is to say, about 310,000 acres. And if we have recourse to maize and practice ensilage (the compression of fodder while green) like Arabs, we obtain fodder on an area of 217,500 acres.

In the environs of Milan, where sewer water is used to irrigate the fields, fodder for 2 to 3 horned cattle per each acre is obtained on an area of 22,000 acres; and on a few favoured fields, up to 177 tons of hay to the 10 acres have been cropped, the yearly provender of 36 milch cows. Nearly nine acres per head of cattle are needed under the pasture system, and only 2½ acres for 9 oxen or cows under the new system. These are the opposite extremes in modern agriculture.

In Guernsey, on a total of 9884 acres utilized, nearly half (4695 acres) are covered with cereals and kitchen-gardens; only 5189 acres remain as meadows. On these 5189 acres, 1480 horses, 7260 head of cattle, 900 sheep, and 4200 pigs are fed, which makes more than 3 head of cattle per 2 acres, without reckoning the sheep or the pigs. It is needless to add that the fertility of the soil is made by seaweed and chemical manures.

Returning to our 3½ million inhabitants belonging to Paris and its environs, we see that the land necessary for the rearing of cattle comes down from 5 million acres to 197,000. Well, then, let us not stop at the lowest figures, let us take those of ordinary intensive culture; let us liberally add to the land necessary for smaller cattle which must replace some of the horned beasts and allow 395,000 acres for the rearing of cattle—494,000 if you like, on the 1,013,000 acres remaining after bread has been provided for the people.

Let us be generous and give 5 million work-days to put this landinto a productive state.

After having therefore employed in the course of a year 20 million work-days, half of which are for permanent improvements, we shall have bread and meat assured to us, without including all the extra meat obtainable in the shape of fowls, pigs, rabbits, etc.; without taking into consideration that a population provided with excellent vegetables and fruit consumes less meat than Englishmen, who supplement their poor supply of vegetables by animal food. Now, how much do 20 million work-days of 5 hours make per inhabitant? Very little indeed. A population of 3½ millions must have at least 1,200,000 adult men, and as many women capable of work. Well, then, to give bread and meat to all, it would need only 17 half-days of work a year per man. Add 3 million work-days, or double that number if you like, in order to obtain milk. That will make 25 work-days of 5 hours in all—nothing more than a little pleasurable country exercise—to obtain the three principal products bread, meat, and milk. The three products which, after housing, cause daily anxiety to nine-tenths of mankind.

And yet—let us not tire of repeating—these are not fancy dreams. We have only told what is, what has been, obtained by experience on a large scale. Agriculture could be reorganized in this way to-morrow if property laws and general ignorance did not offer opposition.

The day Paris has understood that to know what you eat and how it is produced, is a question of public interest; the day when everybody will have understood that this questions is infinitely more important than all the parliamentary debates of the present times—on that day the Revolution will be an accomplished fact. Paris will take possession of the two departments and cultivate them. And then the Parisian worker, after having laboured a third of his existence in order to buy bad and insufficient food, will produce it himself, under his walls, within the enclosure of his forts (if they still exist), in a few hours of healthy and attractive work.

And now we pass on to fruit and vegetables. Let us go outside Paris and visit the establishment of a market-gardener who accomplishes wonders (ignored by learned economists) at a few miles from the academies.

Let us visit, suppose, M. Ponce, the author of a work on market-gardening, who makes no secret of what the earth yields him, and who has published it all along.

M. Ponce, and especially his workmen, work like niggers. It takes eight men to cultivate a plot a little less than 3 acres (27/10). They work 12, and even 15 hours a day, that is to say, three times more than is needed. Twenty-four of them would not be too many. To which M. Ponce will probably answer that as he pays the terrible sum of £100 rent a year for his 27/10 acres of land, and £100 for manure bought in the barracks, he is obliged to exploit. He would no doubt answer, "Being exploited, I exploit in my turn." His installation has also cost him £1200, of which certainly more than half went as tribute to the idle barons of industry. In reality, this establishment represents at most 3000 work-days, probably much less.

But let us examine his crops: nearly 10 tons of carrots, nearly 10 tons of onions, radishes, and small vegetables, 6000 heads of cabbage, 3000 heads of cauliflower, 5000 baskets of tomatoes, 5000 dozen of choice fruit, 154,000 salads; in short, a total of 123 tons of vegetables and fruit to 27/10 acres—120 yards long by 109 yards broad, which makes more than 44 tons of vegetables to the acre.

But a man does not eat more than 660 lb. of vegetables and fruit a year, and 2½ acres of a market-garden yield enough vegetables and fruit to richly supply the table of 350 adults during the year. Thus 24 persons employed a whole year in cultivating 27/10 acres of land, and only working 5 hours a day, would produce sufficient vegetables and fruit for 350 adults, which is equivalent at least to 500 individuals.

To put it in another way: in cultivating like M. Ponce—and his results have already been surpassed—350 adults should each give a little more than 100 hours a year (103) to produce vegetables and fruit necessary for 500 people.

Let us mention that such a production is not the exception. It takes place, under the walls of Paris, on an area of 2220 acres, by 5000 market-gardeners. Only these market-gardeners are reduced nowadays to a state of beasts of burden, in order to pay an average rent of £32 per acre.

But do not these facts, which can be verified by every one, prove that 17,300 acres (of the 519,000 remaining to us) would suffice to give all necessary vegetables, as well as a liberal amount of fruit to the 3½ millions inhabitants of our two departments?

As to the quantity of work necessary to produce these fruits and vegetables, it would amount to 50 million work-days of 5 hours (50 days per adult male), if we measure by the market-gardeners' standard of work. But we could reduce this quantity if we had recourse to the process in vogue in Jersey and Guernsey. We must also remember that the Paris market-gardener is forced to work so hard because he mostly produces early season fruits, the high prices of which have to pay for fabulous rents, and that this system of culture entails more work than is really necessary. The market-gardeners of Paris, not having the means to make a great outlay on their gardens, and being obliged to pay heavily for glass, wood, iron, an coal, obtain their artificial heat out of manure, while it can be had at much less cost in hothouses.

IV

The market-gardeners, we say, are forced to become machines and to renounce all joys of lift to obtain their marvellous crops. But these hard grinders have rendered a great service to humanity in teaching us that the soil can be "made." They make it with old hotbeds of manure, which have already served to give the necessary warmth to young plants and to early fruit; and they make it in such great quantity that they are compelled to sell it in part, otherwise it would raise the level of their gardens by one inch every year. They do it so well (so Barral teaches us, in his "Dictionary of Agriculture," in an article on market-gardeners) that in recent contracts, the market-gardener stipulates that he will carry away his soil with him when he leaves the bit of ground he is cultivating. Loam carried away on carts, with furniture and glass frames—that is the answer of practical cultivators to the learned treatises of a Ricardo, who represented rent as a means of equalizing the natural advantages of the soil. "The soil is worth what man is worth," that is the gardeners' motto.

And yet the market-gardeners of Paris and Rouen labour three times as hard to obtain the same results as their fellow-workers in Guernscy or in England. Applying industry to agriculture these last make their climate in addition to their soil, by means of the greenhouse.

Fifty years ago the greenhouse was the luxury of the rich. It was kept to grow exotic plants for pleasure. But nowadays its use begins to be generalized. A tremendous industry has grown up lately in Guernsey and Jersey, where hundreds of acres are already covered with glass—to say nothing of the countless small greenhouses kept in every little farm garden. Acres and acres of greenhouses have lately been built also at Worthing, in the suburbs of London, and in several other parts of England and Scotland.

They are built of all qualities, beginning with those which have granite walls, down to those which represent mere shelters made in planks and glass frames, which cost, even now, with all the tribute paid to capitalists and middlemen, less than 3s. 6d. per square yard under glass. Most of them are heated for at least three or four months every year; but even the cool greenhouses, which are not heated at all, give excellent results—of course, not for growing grapes and tropical plants, but for potatoes, carrots, peas, tomatoes, and so on.

In this way man emancipates himself from climate, and at the same time he avoids also the heavy work with the hot-beds, and he saves both in buying much less manure and in work. Three men to the acre, each of them working less than sixty hours a week, grow on very small spaces what formerly required acres and acres of land.

The result of all these recent conquests of culture is, that if one half only of the adults of a city gave each about fifty half-days for the culture of the finest fruit and vegetables out of season, they would have all the year round an unlimited supply of that sort of fruit and vegetables for the whole population.

But there is a still more important fact to notice. The greenhouse has nowadays a tendency to become a mere *kitchen garden under glass*. And when it is used to such a purpose, the simplest plank-and-glass unheated shelters already give fabulous crops—such as, for instance, 500 bushels of potatoes per acre as a first crop, ready by the end of April; after which a second and a third crop are obtained in the extremely high temperature which prevails in the summer under glass.

I gave in my "Fields, Factories, and Workshops," most striking facts in this direction. Sufficient to say here, that at Jersey, 34 men, with one trained gardener only, cultivate 13 acres under glass, from which they obtain 143 tons of fruit and early vegetables, using for this extraordinary culture less than 1000 tons of coal.

And this is done now in Guernsey and Jersey on a very large scale, quite a number of steamers constantly plying between Guernsey and London, only to export the crops of the greenhouses.

Nowadays, in order to obtain that same crop of 500 bushels of potatoes, we must plough every year a surface of 4 acres, plant it, cultivate it, weed it, and so on; whereas with the glass, even if we shall have to give perhaps, to start with, half a day's work per square yard in order to build the greenhouse—we shall save afterwards at least one-half, and probably three-quarters of the formerly required yearly labour.

These are *facts,* results which every one can verify himself. And these facts are already a hint as to what man could obtain from the earth if he treated it with intelligence.

V

In all the above we have reasoned upon what already withstood the test of experience. Intensive culture of the fields, irrigated meadows, the hothouse, and finally the kitchen garden under glass are realities. Moreover, the tendency is to extend and to generalize these methods of culture, because they allow of obtaining more produce with less work and with more certainty.

In fact, after having studied the most simple glass shelters of Guernsey, we affirm that, taking all in all, far less work is expended for obtaining potatoes under glass in April, than in growing them in the open air, which requires digging a space four times as large, watering it, weeding it, etc. Work is likewise economized in employing a perfected tool or machine, even when an initial expense had to be incurred to buy the tool.

Complete figures concerning the culture of common vegetables under glass are still wanting. This culture is of recent origin, and is only carried out on small areas. But we have already figures concerning the fifty years old culture of early season grapes, and these figures are conclusive.

In the north of England, on the Scotch frontier, where coal only costs 3s. a ton at the pit's mouth, they have long since taken to growing hothouse grapes. Thirty years ago these grapes, ripe in January, were sold by the grower at 20s. per lb. and resold at 40s. per lb. for Napoleon III's table. To-day the same grower sells them at only 2s. 6d. per lb. He tells us so himself in a horticultural journal. The fall is caused by tons and tons of grapes arriving in January to London and Paris.

Thanks to the cheapness of coal and an intelligent culture, grapes from the north travel now southwards, in a contrary direction to ordinary fruit. They cost so little that in May, English and Jersey grapes are sold at 1s. 8d. per lb. by the gardeners, and yet this price, like that of 40s. thirty years ago, is only kept up by slack production.

In March, Belgium grapes are sold at from 6d. to 8d., while in October, grapes cultivated in immense quantities—under glass, and with a little artificial heating in the environs of London—are sold at the same price as grapes bought by the pound in the vineyards of Switzerland and the Rhine, that is to say, for a few halfpence. Yet they still cost two-thirds too much, by reason of the excessive rent of the soil and the cost of installation and heating, on which the gardener pays a formidable tribute to the manufacturer and middleman. This being understood, we may say that it costs "next to nothing" to have delicious grapes under the latitude of, and in our misty London in autumn. In one of the suburbs, for instance, a wretched glass and plaster shelter, 9 ft. 10 in. long by 6½ ft. wide, resting against our cottage, gave us about fifty pounds of grapes of an exquisite taste in October, for nine consecutive years. The crop came from a Hamburg vine-stalk, six years old. And the shelter was so bad that the rain came through. At night the temperature was always that of outside. It was evidently not heated, for that would be as useless as to heat the street! And the cares to be given were: pruning the vine half an hour every year; and bringing a wheelbarrowful of manure, which is thrown over the stalk of the vine, planted in red clay outside the shelter.

On the other hand, if we estimate the amount of care given to the vine on the borders of the Rhine or Lake Leman, the terraces constructed stone upon stone on the slopes of the hills, the transport of manure and also of earth to a height of two or three hundred feet, we come to the conclusion that on the whole the expenditure of work necessary to cultivate vines is more considerable in Switzerland or on the banks of the Rhine than it is under glass in London suburbs.

This may seem paradoxical, because it is generally believed that vines grow of themselves in the south of Europe, and that the vinegrower's work costs nothing. But gardeners and horticulturists, far from contradicting us, confirm our assertions. "The most advantageous culture in England is vine culture," wrote a practical gardener, editor of the "English Journal of Horticulture." Prices speak eloquently for themselves, as we know.

Translating these facts into communist language, we may assert that the man or woman who takes twenty hours a year from his leisure time to give some little care—very pleasant in the main—to two or three vine-stalks sheltered by simple glass under any European climate, will gather as many grapes as their family and friends can eat. And that applies not only to vines, but to all fruit trees.

The Commune that will put the processes of intensive culture into practice on a large scale will have all possible vegetables, indigenous or exotic, and all desirable fruits, without employing more than about ten hours a year per inhabitant.

In fact, nothing would be easier than to verify the above statements by direct experiment. Suppose 100 acres of a light loam (such as we have at Worthing) are transformed into a number of market gardens, each one with its glass houses for the rearing of the seedlings and young plants. Suppose also that 50 more acres are covered with glass, houses, and the organization of the whole is left to practical experienced French *maraichers,* and Guernsey or Worthing greenhouse gardeners.

In basing the maintenance of these 150 acres on the Jersey average, requiring the work of three men per acre under glass—which makes less than 8,600 hours of work a year—it would need about 1,300,000 hours for the 150 acres. Fifty competent gardeners could give five hours a day to this work, and the rest would be simply done by people who, without being gardeners by profession, would soon learn how to use a spade, and to handle the plants. But this work would yield at least—we have seen it in a preceding chapter—all necessaries and articles of luxury in the way of fruit and vegetables for at least 40,000 or 50,000 people. Let us admit that among this number there are 13,500 adults, willing to work at the kitchen-garden; then, each one would have to give 100 hours a year distributed over the whole year. These hours of work would become hours of recreation spent among friends and children in beautiful gardens, more beautiful probably than those of the legendary Semiramis.

This is the balance sheet of the labour to be spent in order to be able to eat to satiety fruit which we are deprived of to-day, and to have vegetables in abundance, now so scrupulously rationed out by the housewife, when she has to reckon each halfpenny which must go to enrich capitalists and landowners (2).

If only humanity had the consciousness of what it CAN, and if that consciousness only gave it the power to will!

If it only knew that cowardice of the spirit is the rock on which all revolutions have stranded until now.

VI

We can easily perceive the new horizons opening before the social revolution.

Each time we speak of revolution the worker who has seen children wanting food lowers his brow and repeats obstinately—"What of bread? Will there be sufficient if everyone eats according to his appetite? What if the peasants, ignorant tools of reaction, starve our towns as the black bands did in France in 1793—what shall we do?"

Let them do their worst! The large cities will have to do without them.

At what, then, should the hundreds of thousands of workers, who are asphyxiated to-day in small workshops and factories, be employed on the day they regain their liberty? Will they continue locking themselves up in factories after the Revolution? Will they continue to make luxurious toys for export when they see their stock of corn getting exhausted, meat becoming scarce, and vegetables disappearing without being replaced?

Evidently not! They will leave the town and go into the fields! Aided by a machinery which will enable the weakest of us to put a shoulder to the wheel, they will carry revolution into previously enslaved culture as they will have carried it into institutions and ideas.

Hundreds of acres will be covered with glass, and men, and women with delicate fingers, will foster the growth of young plants. Hundreds of other acres will be ploughed by steam, improved by manures, or enriched by artificial soil obtained by the pulverization of rocks. Happy crowds of occasional labourers will cover these acres with crops, guided in the work and experiments partly by those who know agriculture, but especially by the great and practical spirit of a people roused from long slumber and illumined by that bright beacon—the happiness of all.

And in two or three months the early crops will relieve the most pressing wants, and provide food for a people who, after so many centuries of expectation, will at least be able to appease their hunger and eat according to their appetite.

In the meanwhile, popular genius, the genius of a nation which revolts and knows its wants, will work at experimenting with new processes of culture that we already catch a glimpse of, and that only need the baptism of experience to become universal. Light will be experimented with—that unknown agent of culture which makes barley ripen in forty-five days under the latitude of Yakutsk; light, concentrated or artificial, will rival heat in hastening the growth of plants. A Mouchot of the future will invent a machine to guide the rays of the sun and make them work, so that we shall no longer seek sun-heat stored in coal in the depths of the earth. They will experiment the watering of the soil with cultures of micro-organisms—a rational idea, conceived but yesterday, which will permit us to give to the soil those little living beings, necessary to feed the rootless, to decompose and assimilate the component parts of the soil.

They will experiment.... But let us stop here or we shall enter into the realm of fancy. Let us remain in the reality of acquired facts. With the processes of culture in use, applied on a large scale, and already victorious in the struggle against industrial competition, we can give ourselves ease and luxury in return for agreeable work. The near future will show what is practical in the processes that recent scientific discoveries give us a glimpse of. Let us limit ourselves at present to opening up the new path that consists in *the study of the needs of man, and the means of satisfying them.*

The only thing that may be wanting to the Revolution is the boldness of initiative.

With our minds already narrowed in our youth, enslaved by the past in our mature age and till the grave, we hardly dare to think. If a new idea is mentioned—before venturing on an opinion of our own, we consult musty books a hundred years old, to know what ancient masters thought on the subject.

It is not food that will fail, if boldness of thought and initiative are not wanting to the revolution.

Of all the great days of the French Revolution, the most beautiful, the greatest, was the one on which delegates who had come from all parts of France to Paris, worked all with the spade to plane the ground of the Champ de Mars, preparing it for the fÃªte of the Federation.

That day France was united: animated by the new spirit, she had a vision of the future in the working in common of the soil.

And it will again be by the working in common of the soil that the enfranchized societies will find their unity and will obliterate hatred and oppression which had divided them.

Henceforth, able to conceive solidarity—that immense power which increases man's energy and creative forces a hundredfold—the new society will march to the conquest of the future with all the vigour of youth.

Leaving off production for unknown buyers, and looking in its midst for needs and tastes to be satisfied, society will liberally assure the life and ease of each of its members, as well as that moral satisfaction which work gives when freely chosen and freely accomplished, and the joy of living without encroaching on the life of others.

Inspired by a new daring—thanks to the sentiment of solidarity—all will march together to the conquest of the high joys of knowledge and artistic creation.

A society thus inspired will fear neither dissensions within nor enemies without. To the coalitions of the past it will oppose a new harmony, the initiative of each and all, the daring which springs from the awakening of a people's genius.

Before such an irresistible force "conspiring kings" will be powerless. Nothing will remain for them but to bow before it, and to harness themselves to the chariot of humanity, rolling towards new horizons opened up by the Social Revolution.

NOTES

(1) Consult "La Repartition metrique des imp6ts," by A. Toubeau, two vols., published by GuiUaumin in 1880. (We do not in the least agree with Toubeau's conclusions, but it is a real encyclopaedia, indicating the sources which prove what can be obtained from the soil.) " La Culture maraichere," by M. Ponce, Paris, 1869. " Le Potager Gressent," Paris, 1885, an excellent practical work. " Physiologie et culture du ble," by Risler, Paris, 1881. " Le ble, sa culture intensive et extensive," by Lecouteux, Paris, 1883. "La Cite Chinoise," by Eugene Simon. "Le dictionnaire d'agriculture," by Barral (Hachette, editor). " The Rothamstead Experiments," by Wm. Fream, London, 1888—culture without manure, etc. (the "Field" office, editor). "Fields, Factories, and Workshops," by the author. London (Swan Sonnenschein) ; cheap editions at 6d. and is.

(2) Summing up the figures given on agriculture, figures proving that the inhabitants of the two departements of Seine and Seine-et-Oise can perfectly weU live on their own territory by employing very Httle time annually to obtain food, we have : —

Departments of Seine and Seine-et-Oise

Number of inhabitants in 1889	3,900,000
Area in acres	1,507,300
Average number of inhabitants per acre .	2-6
Areas to be cultivated to feed the inhabitants (inacres) :—	
Corn and cereals	494,000
Natural and artificial meadows	494,000
Vegetables and fruit from	17,300 to 25,000
Leaving a balance for houses, roads, parks, forests	494,000

Quantity of annual work necessary to improve and cultivate the above surfaces in five-hour work-days :—

Cereals (culture and crop)	15,000,000
Meadows, milk, rearing of cattle	10,000,000
Market-gardening culture, high-class fruit	33,000,000
Extras	12,000,000
Total	70,000,000

If we suppose that half only of the able-bodied adults (men and women) are willing to work at agriculture, we see that 70 million work-days must be divided among 1,200,000 individuals, which gives us 58 work-days of 5 hours for each of these workers. With that the population of the two departments would have aU necessary bread, meat, milk, vegetables, and fruit, both ordinary and luxury. To-day a workman spends for the necessary food of his family (generally less than what is necessary) at least one-third of his 300 work-days a year, about 1000 hours be it, instead of 290. That is, he thus gives about 700 hours too much to fatten the idle and the would-be administrators, because he does not produce his ovm food, but buys it of middlemen, who in their turn buy it of peasants who exhaust themselves by working with bad tools, because, being robbed by the landowners and the State, they cannot procure better ones.